MORE THAN PETTICOATS

Remarkable
MISSOURI WOMEN

MORE THAN PETTICOATS

Remarkable
MISSOURI WOMEN

Elaine Warner

Guilford, Connecticut

To buy books in quantity for corporate use
or incentives, call **(800) 962-0973**
or e-mail **premiums@GlobePequot.com**.

Map by Daniel Lloyd © Morris Book Publishing, LLC
Project editor: Meredith Dias
Layout: Sue Murray

Library of Congress Cataloging-in-Publication Data
Warner, Elaine.
 More than petticoats. Remarkable Missouri women / Elaine Warner.
    p. cm.
 Includes bibliographical references and index.
 ISBN 978-0-7627-6397-9
 1. Women—Missouri—Biography. 2. Women—Missouri—History. 3.
Missouri—Biography. I. Title. II. Title: Remarkable Missouri women.
 CT3262.M8W37 2012
 920.72—dc23

                                                2011039925

Printed in the United States of America
10 9 8 7 6 5 4 3 2 1

CONTENTS

IOWA

Missouri River

Kansas River

Edina

Mississippi River

ILLINOIS

Missouri River

INDEPENDENCE

KANSAS
CITY

JEFFERSON
CITY

OTTERVILLE

St. Louis

KANSAS

NEVADA

SPRINGFIELD

BONNIEBROOK   MANSFIELD

MISSOURI

MELVA   FORSYTH
KIRBYVILLE

OKLAHOMA

TENNESSEE

ARKANSAS

0   50   50 kilometers
0   50   50 miles

N

ACKNOWLEDGMENTS

To paraphrase President Harry Truman, the book stops here. I get my name on the title page, but I certainly didn't write this all on my own. It took lots of people with infinite patience and special knowledge—finding sources, locating photographs, and answering innumerable questions.

Among those individuals and institutions to whom I owe thanks are:

The Missouri History Museum Library, St. Louis—Emily Jaycox, who was at work before I arrived to make sure the books I needed were available, saved me valuable time on much too short a visit. Carol Verble showed me the ropes, Edna Smith kept the copying machine busy for me, Dennis Northcutt helped me with the archives, and Jaime Bourassa found needed photos for me.

The Missouri Valley Room of the Kansas City Public Library was a treasure trove of information. The staff couldn't have been more accommodating.

Ronna Davis and the research crew at the Edmond Public Library helped me locate books through interlibrary loan.

Matt Reitzel at the South Dakota State Historical Society, Jennifer Laughlin at the Wyandotte County Historical Museum, David Boutros at the State Historical Society of Missouri Research Center, Kansas City, and Lisa Keys at the Kansas State Historical Society all helped me look for photos.

Greg Goss, assistant to the director of the Laura Ingalls Wilder Home Association in Mansfield, Missouri, did yeoman service in obtaining the photo of Laura.

Susan K. Scott was a gracious hostess during my visit to the Rose O'Neill Museum and Bonniebrook, and her own scholarship added many brushstrokes to the picture of Rose O'Neill.

The Ralph Foster Museum at the College of the Ozarks was an excellent resource on local history and the remarkable women of the area. Thanks to Annette Sain at the museum and Gwen Simmons at the Lyons Memorial Library at the college.

Nancy Piepenbring, manuscript specialist at the Western Historical Manuscript Collection at the University of Missouri at Kansas City, used her research skills to ferret out an obscure piece of information for the chapter on Nell Donnelly.

At Cottey College, Nancy Kerbs, Director of Assessment and Institutional Research, provided lots of information on both the founder and the school, while Linda Russell sent me a selection of photos of Virginia Alice Cottey Stockard.

After many failed attempts to locate a particular biography of Virginia Alice Cottey Stockard, I mentioned my frustration to a PEO (Philanthropic Educational Organization) International member at church one Sunday. "I think I have it," she told me. And she did. Thanks, Jo Jackson.

Cathy Williams, as the least known of my subjects, presented a problem when it came to getting a photo. Kansas City artist William Jennings had painted a portrait of her based on written description and military information. I greatly appreciate his providing me with the image for her chapter and Commander Carlton Philpot of the Buffalo Soldier Educational and Historical Committee for their permission to use it.

Meeting Mary Jo Kirkey, Mary Elizabeth Mahnkey's granddaughter, was a real treat. I loved listening to her memories of her grandmother.

Ellen Gray Massey, Mary Elizabeth Mahnkey, biographer, shared information and added encouragement.

Jace Land, grandson of photographer Townsend Godsey, provided Mary Elizabeth's photo.

Terence Michael O'Malley provided not only a lively and interesting biography (*A Stitch in Time*) of his great-great aunt, Nell Donnelly, but also her photograph.

Barbara Mueth, vice president of community relations for Children's Mercy Hospital in Kansas City, sent copies of hard-to-find material, including an unpublished manuscript about Alice Graham, Kate Richardson, and the early days of the hospital. Telisa Hassen, the public relations manager, sent pictures.

Mary Hendron of Insight Marketing and Communication is my source for all things St. Louis. If she doesn't know an answer, she knows who does.

Thanks to friends Gladys Dronberger and Phyllis Jarrett, who read several of the chapters, caught typos, and made suggestions that improved the writing.

I can't say enough about my daughter, Zoe McAden, who read the rest of the manuscript; she's my toughest critic but always gentle about the way she does it.

My husband of half a century, Jack, put up with my odd hours, erratic meals, and occasional whining.

And, of course, thanks to those remarkable women at Globe Pequot: Meredith Rufino, Erin Turner, Ellen Urban, and Meredith Dias. Thanks also to copyeditor Colleen Sell. I never could have done this without all of you.

INTRODUCTION

From the earliest days of Missouri's history, women have helped give the "Show Me" state lots to show. But they often didn't get the credit.

There have always been women who forged their own way, in spite of social pressures—sometimes working within the system, sometimes working despite the system. The thirteen women in this book were chosen for their talents, perseverance, and ingenuity. Many more could have been selected.

The women reflect a broad spectrum of activities. Six of them taught school at one time or another, although only two made education their life's work. Six were published writers: for three of them writing was a secondary achievement. The professions of law and medicine are represented, with two practitioners each. One woman is known primarily as an artist, another as a business woman and a third as an entertainer. One of the women was known as a man for several years of her life.

Though not common to all the women, a supportive family was a big factor in the success of a number of them. Many of the women also seem to have shared a love of and emphasis on reading.

Two of the women never married, and only two had marriages that lasted many years. Several of the women discovered that being a widow allowed them freedom and rights that other woman did not have. Four of the women were divorced—distinctly shocking in their time. The nineteenth and early twentieth centuries were tough times for women; there were physical challenges for women on the frontier, societal challenges in attitudes towards women and their roles, and legal barriers to personal and financial autonomy for females. In addition to the restrictions imposed on women in general, two of the subjects shouldered the extra burden of racial prejudice.

Reading about the lives of women in the past makes it hard to be too nostalgic for "the good old days." Instead, it should make us grateful for those pioneers who paved the way for the women of today.

PHOEBE COUZINS

(1842–1913)

SUFFRAGIST: PROPONENT AND ADVERSARY

Phoebe Couzins's life was one of radical contradictions. She was among the most passionate advocates of the Women's Suffrage Movement, yet she made a 180-degree turn in her thinking toward the end of her life. An early supporter of Prohibition and a lecturer on the evils of drink, she later became a lobbyist for the United Brewers Association. Although she was the first woman to graduate from law school in Missouri, she was not the first female lawyer in the state. During her life she made many friends—and many enemies. Born in prominence, she died in poverty and obscurity. She was fascinating and infuriating but nonetheless a brilliant and tireless worker for women's rights.

Her father, John Edward Decker Couzins, was born in England but immigrated to America with his family when he was a child. He trained to become an architect and builder in New York City, where he met and married Adaline Weston. The couple moved to St. Louis in 1834.

Birthdates for Phoebe vary widely—from 1839 to 1845. The date on her tombstone, erected some years after her death, is 1842; the 1850 and 1860 censuses indicate 1841. Little is known about her childhood and early education.

We start to learn more about Phoebe during the Civil War period. During that time, her father served as the St. Louis chief of police and acting provost marshal of Missouri. He also served as the head of a small group of citizens called the Committee of Safety, which worked hard to keep the state from seceding from the Union.

Her mother was a woman ahead of her time. When the war began, she volunteered to assist a civilian surgeon who worked for the Union

Phoebe Couzins Courtesy of the Missouri Historical Museum, St. Louis

army. At first, her job consisted of making bandages and dressing wounds of soldiers who were brought to St. Louis. Later, she accompanied the doctor across Missouri to the battlefields in the southwestern part of the state. As the war raged on, their services were needed in Tennessee and Mississippi, where they set up hospital ships on steamboats to treat casualties of the Battles of Shiloh and Vicksburg. In pursuit of her duties, Adaline suffered frostbite and even a gunshot wound. Following her return to St. Louis, she continued with her war work aided by her daughter Phoebe. With such an intrepid mother and civically active father, no wonder Phoebe considered a less-than-traditional path for her life.

After the war, both Adaline and Phoebe became involved with the growing women's suffrage movement. Phoebe saw the inequalities in society and the low status of women and railed against the ignorance and powerlessness in which women were kept. She articulated her feelings in a later speech,

> *I am glad to welcome any and all movements which tend to lift woman out of her narrow, traditional life, and place her upon her feet where she may think and act for herself. Hitherto, the doctrine of self-reliance, self-culture, personal responsibility, has never been taught to woman; she has been regarded as created for man's self-love alone, without individual accountability to render her Maker, and thus the race has slowly, painfully climbed the heights of progress, dragging a dead weight, securely manacled at feet and wrists, which its own hands have forged.*

Stung by these injustices, Phoebe Couzins requested admission to the Washington University School of Law in St. Louis. The law school faculty members issued a statement, ". . . the Law Faculty see no reason why any young woman who in respect to character and acquirements fulfilled the Conditions applicable to male Students, and who chose to attend the Law Lectures in good faith for the purpose of becoming acquainted with the laws of her country, should be denied that privilege." The university's board of directors concurred, and Phoebe Couzins was admitted, making Washington University the first law school in the country to admit students regardless of gender.

About the same time, the school received a request of admission from a Miss Lemma Barkaloo. Both women became students at the school. Their entrance was well received by their fellow students, a fact acknowledged by Phoebe, who later said, "If, as a woman, I was not welcome in the class, the students have never manifested it by word, look or deed."

Miss Barkaloo did not complete her courses nor graduate; however, she took and passed the bar examination, becoming Missouri's first female lawyer. Phoebe became the country's first female law school graduate. She was subsequently admitted to practice in the states of Missouri, Kansas, Utah, Arkansas, the Dakota Territories, and the federal courts.

Phoebe set up a small law office in downtown St. Louis, but practicing law was not her primary goal. Tall and thin with a mass of dark hair and deep-set eyes, she was a commanding speaker and advocate for women's rights.

She had always been clear about her intentions. In the speech given at a grand dinner celebrating her graduation in 1871, she told the guests:

> *Two years ago I entered upon the study of the law with many forebodings, toned with many conflicts and doubts as to its expediency, yet, actuated solely by a desire to open new paths for woman, enlarge her usefulness, widen her responsibilities and to plead her cause in a struggle which I believed was surely coming. . . . [L]et me say that I trust the day is not far distant, when men and women shall be recognized as equal administrators of that great bulwark of civilization, law.*

Even before leaving law school, Phoebe, a member of the Woman Suffrage Association of Missouri (WSAM), exercised her oratorical skills in the cause. In 1869, she testified before the Missouri legislature on the subject of votes for women. The plea fell on unsympathetic ears; Missouri did not allow women to vote until the Nineteenth Amendment to the US Constitution was ratified in 1920.

The women's suffrage movement began in Seneca Falls, New York, in 1848, when Elizabeth Cady Stanton, Lucretia Mott, Martha Wright, Mary Ann McClintock, and Jane Hunt met to plan the first women's rights convention. They prepared a document, "A Declaration of Sentiments," based on the Declaration of Independence. In it they called for equality for women in education and employment, equitable property rights, and the right to vote for women.

In 1869, a division of opinion occurred among followers of the founders, and the movement split into two camps—the National Woman Suffrage Association (NWSA) and the American Woman Suffrage Association (AWSA). The NWSA, led by Elizabeth Cady Stanton and Susan B. Anthony, was considered more radical than the AWSA. When the Missouri group chose to go with the more conservative group, Phoebe left the organization but not the cause. The NWSA opposed ratification of the Fifteenth Amendment giving black men the right to vote—not because they opposed black men but because women were not included.

Phoebe, who at this time was contributing articles to *The Revolution*, a weekly publication edited by Stanton and published by Anthony, wrote, "I regard it was neither just nor generous to eternally compel women to yield on all questions . . . simply because they are *women*."

Presumably enabled by her father's financial backing, Phoebe traveled to other parts of the country to give speeches on women's rights. In 1874, she spoke before the national convention of the NWSA in Washington, DC, the first of four times she would address the national group.

She often traveled with Stanton and Anthony to meet with groups of women around the nation.

The Women's Christian Temperance Union (WCTU) was founded in 1874 in Ohio and became a great political force. Phoebe served as an important voice for that movement, too. The WCTU cause was entwined with the suffrage question in that it brought the liquor lobbyists out in force to protest against votes for women and to object to any tightening of liquor laws. These men felt that if women were allowed to vote, they would most likely vote against free-flowing alcohol.

Phoebe continued to receive accolades for her speaking abilities. She also had other abilities with which she occasionally wowed the crowds that heard her speak. In 1878, while visiting a friend in Whitewater, Minnesota, she was invited to participate in a temperance rally. During the Sunday evening meeting, she rose and sang two solos that were described as having "a great deal of sweetness and power." She was invited back the next night to speak to the group. More than three thousand people crowded into the tent to hear her. She spoke for two hours, holding her audience in her hands. Listeners were so impressed that she was invited back to give the commencement address at the local teachers' college.

Phoebe's successes gained her national attention. In addition to speaking at NWSA conventions, she was the first woman to speak at a national political convention. The 1876 Democratic National Convention was held in St. Louis—the first time a national political convention had ever been held west of the Mississippi. On behalf of NWSA, Phoebe was allowed to address the assembly and request that a plank seeking votes for women be added to the national platform. Though she spoke eloquently, it took forty years and ten conventions before that happened.

Phoebe's abilities as an orator, combined with her legal education, made her a formidable figure. A lesser lady might have been intimidated by testifying before the US Congress. Phoebe was not. Suffragist leader Elizabeth Cady Stanton said that while Phoebe had never practiced as an attorney, "the knowledge and discipline acquired in the study of our American system of jurisprudence and constitutional law have been of essential service to her in the prolonged arguments on the enfranchisement of woman."

Able to see through the labyrinth of legal arguments against women voting, Phoebe rebutted those with twists of her own. One of the cases she pored over was the 1874 US Supreme Court finding in *Minor v. Happersett*.

Virginia Minor, a citizen of Missouri, had attempted to register to vote in the national election of 1872. She was turned away by the registrar because the constitution of the state of Missouri stated "every male citizen of the United States shall be entitled to vote." Stating the obvious, that Miss Minor was not male, he refused to register her. She sued.

The case went all the way to the US Supreme Court, where the justices deliberated and then upheld the ban on registration in a lengthy opinion. They began with a rambling dissertation on what "citizen" means—for example, who is a citizen and how does someone who is not a citizen become a citizen? From there, they segued into a discussion of the US Constitution and the constitutions of the various states. They pointed out differences in voting requirements and how, in one state, it was even possible to vote before becoming a citizen. They stressed that when the original colonies banded together, each entity had its own constitution, which they were allowed to keep. They stressed that voting was not a right of citizenship.

The conclusion was: "Being unanimously of the opinion that the Constitution of the United States does not confer the right of suffrage upon any one, and that the constitutions and laws of the several States which commit that important trust to men alone are not necessarily void, we affirm the judgment."

Phoebe brought up the Minor case when, in 1880, she testified before the House Judiciary Committee. She excoriated the decision, saying, "[T]he rights of one-half of the people were deliberately abrogated without a dissenting voice." She went on to argue—after the fact and to no avail—that under that argument, the federal government had no authority to grant voting rights under the Fifteenth Amendment, and therefore, in effect, no authority over the states, which made the Civil War a sham and an exercise in futility. In spite of seeing little success, Phoebe continued to fight against inequality.

Her persistence and her public appearances won her admirers—and detractors. In 1882, her name was put forth to President Chester A. Arthur as a candidate for the commission that oversaw the affairs of the Utah Territory. It was a good choice. Her legal background would have served her well, and she had been admitted to the bar in Utah ten years before. She didn't, however, get the job.

A St. Louis newspaper, the *Spectator,* was no fan of feminism or of Phoebe Couzins. It reported:

> *The* Spectator *has a very high respect for Miss Phoebe Cozzens [so high the writer misspelled her name!], a lady who has earned a wide reputation as a strenuous advocate of a doctrine that is as absurd and impractical in sociology as it is in politics. . . . Earnest people are always deserving of respect, although there were cases on record where one was so earnest that he went crazy. . . .*

> *There has been a vast amount said about the capabilities of women as lawyers and it is unquestionably true that they may become very learned in the theory of the law . . . but they are totally unfit to enter into the courts and practice law, and the very fact Miss Cozzens and the others of her sex who have attempted it do not meet with any encouragement of success is the best proof that*

can be afforded. They have the privilege but they make no use of
it for the very simple and plain reasons that the general public
does not want them in any such capacity and because such work
is repugnant to their own habits and tastes.

Two years later, Phoebe's father was appointed US marshal for the Eastern District of Missouri. Phoebe began working with him as his chief clerk. As marshal, her father was the federal government's chief enforcement officer. Upon his death in 1887, Phoebe was appointed by President Grover Cleveland to fill her father's unexpired term. She carried out her duties faithfully, even working to catch counterfeiters and other criminals. She was obviously proud of the position—the first female marshal in US history—and asked that when she died, she be buried wearing her marshal's badge.

Her father's death left Phoebe and her mother with financial difficulties. With her legal skills, Phoebe was able to get a small pension—thirty dollars a month—from the War Department for her mother's service in the Civil War. Because Adaline was a volunteer, this was highly irregular; however, her service had been so outstanding that a special act of Congress was passed in order to grant this recognition of her efforts.

By 1889, Phoebe had moved to Washington, DC and was writing articles for newspapers and magazines. In 1890, she was offered a paid position as secretary to the Board of Lady Managers for the World's Columbian Commission working on the 1892 Chicago World's Fair. She needed the money but found herself in conflict with some of the other members. She was fired from her position, and she subsequently sued but lost.

This seems to be the beginning of an increasingly turbulent period in Phoebe's life. She gave an interview to the *New York Times* and spoke bitterly about the treatment she had received in Chicago. She accused officials of conspiring against her and manipulating other committee members.

She also made a startling turnaround in her loyalties toward the suffrage movement. Some writers have suggested she was bitter about the younger, affluent members who had taken over the movement. For whatever reason, she began to withdraw from her position as a spokesperson for the cause, and by 1897 she was speaking and writing against votes for women.

About the same time, she denounced her previous position on alcohol. This was possibly a chicken-and-egg situation. Did she turn against temperance and then accept a job as lobbyist for United Brewers' Association, or did she accept the job and change her opinion to match her position? She held that job for several years before again parting company on bad terms. In letters to the governor of Missouri and President William Taft, she accused company officials of stealing her pension.

She definitely suffered from chronic arthritis, which caused her a great deal of pain. Even with the use of crutches or a wheelchair, she had great difficulty getting around. Her financial situation was also precarious. By 1909 she had returned to St. Louis, where she lived in poverty, possibly preferring to live independently rather than become a charity case.

She died, bitter and alone, in 1913. Still, a spark of the feisty feminist remained. She told her brother, "If I can get back to Washington, John, and get to work again, things will be all right."

If this were a fairy tale, it would have a happier ending. But it was real life, and real people are often complicated. It would be a shame to allow the last few years of Phoebe Couzins' life to negate her accomplishments. She was a woman of firsts: first female law graduate in Missouri, first woman to address a national political convention, and first female marshal. She chose a difficult path and walked it with determination. She opened doors and broke new ground for women. The years she spent fighting for the rights of women deserve to be recognized and celebrated.

SUSAN ELIZABETH BLOW

(1843–1916)

MOTHER OF THE KINDERGARTEN

"Oh my, this will never do," Susan Blow exclaimed as she walked into her brand new kindergarten classroom. The room looked sterile. The walls were blank and the desks were arranged in neat rows. Susan had been in New York completing special training that would prepare her to teach young children in the manner advocated by German educator Friedrich Froebel. The finishing touches had been put on the new Des Peres School while she was away.

It didn't take Susan long to transform the classroom into an appealing, child-friendly space. She replaced the desks with low tables and benches. She decorated the walls and blackboards with pretty colors and pictures. Window sills sported pots of flowers and other plants. She put the "garten" into kindergarten.

Born on June 7, 1843, to Henry Taylor Blow and Minerva Grimsley Blow, Susan Elizabeth Blow was the oldest of a number of children. (Sources vary from six to ten. Quite possibly several of the children died in infancy or early childhood.) The family lived a block from the St. Louis riverfront—just about where the Arch stands today.

In May 1849, the steamboat *White Cloud* was docked a few blocks upriver at the foot of Cherry Street when a fire erupted on the boat and quickly spread through the vessel. The river was lined with steamboats, and the fire jumped from one boat to another. Sparks flew toward the docks, which soon were aflame. Before the fire was put out, it had consumed twenty-three steamboats and one-third of the town, including the Blow's home.

Following the fire, new ordinances were enacted calling for brick or stone buildings in the area, but many residents, fearing another

Susan Elizabeth Blow Courtesy of the Missouri Historical Museum, St. Louis

conflagration, moved to communities west and south of the city. The Blows built a new home in the little French settlement of Carondelet, five miles to the south. Surrounded by seventeen acres, it was a spacious home, which they called "Old Southampton," named after the county in Virginia where the family had previously owned a plantation.

The Blow family was large, and many of Susan's aunts and uncles lived in the area. Her parents had a happy marriage, and the children felt loved and protected. The Blows were well-to-do, affording their children many opportunities other children didn't have.

Unlike many parents of the times, the Blows were dedicated to the education of all their children, not just the boys. Travel played a large part in Susan's education. She had several different governesses; attended classes in arithmetic, reading, French, and grammar in New Orleans; and spent much time reading in her father's library. Henry wrote Minerva in 1857, "I would be extremely happy if we could decide what is best to be done for the English Education of our dear Susie. . . . Sue must have the best advantage in education."

Henry Blow was a successful businessman and president of his company, and in this position he was required to travel frequently. Several of his trips took him to New York City, where he had the opportunity to visit a number of schools. On one of these trips, he took Susan with him to meet Miss Henrietta Haines, who ran an exclusive, private school for girls.

Both father and daughter must have been impressed, because Susan began her studies there in 1858. Susan's solid early education made her a challenge to Miss Haines, and Susan was occasionally frustrated with her teacher's shortcomings. Overall, however, the experience was positive enough that Susan arrived back at school the next term with her younger sister Nellie accompanying her.

Politically, the nation was becoming more divided over the issue of slavery. Although Missouri was a slave state, not everyone in the state agreed with the policy. Henry was one of the founders of the Republican Party in Missouri, and their state platform called for an end to the expansion of slavery. Chosen as a delegate to the 1860 Republican National Convention in Chicago, he and the other Missouri delegates, after giving token support to a "favorite son" candidate, threw their votes to the nomination of Abraham Lincoln. Minerva wrote to her daughters at school:

> We all feel so sad about the state of the country. Even your dear father who is naturally so buoyant is at times depressed. . . . Here in Missouri where a number are identified with slave interest, we who differ with them politically are made to feel the alienation of feeling, and it is not always as pleasant as it ought to be to visit our old friends.

For Henry Blow to take the position he did is interesting because his father, Peter, brought slaves with him to Missouri in 1830. One of the slaves was Dred Scott. After Peter's death, Scott was sold to a Doctor Emerson, who became a surgeon in the US Army. In this capacity, he moved to posts in "free" areas. After his death, Emerson's wife, Irene, returned to Missouri.

In March, 1846, Dred and his wife, Harriet, sued Irene Emerson for their freedom based on their periods of residence in Illinois and Wisconsin Territory, places where slavery was prohibited. Members of the Blow family, including Henry, supported the Scotts in their efforts. The case dragged on and on through the courts, going from the local court up through the Missouri Supreme Court all the way to the United State Supreme Court. A majority of the justices came from slave-holding families, and seven of the nine had been appointed by pro-slavery presidents. Chief Justice Roger Taney from Maryland wrote the majority opinion, which stated that since Dred Scott was a

Negro, he was not a citizen and therefore not entitled to sue. It had taken eleven years to reach that decision.

In the meantime, Mrs. Emerson had remarried. Her new husband, an abolitionist congressman from Massachusetts, was embarrassed to learn his wife owned the most famous slave in the country. He immediately transferred ownership to Taylor Blow, Henry's brother, who freed the Scotts.

According to Nellie's grandson, even though several members of the family helped with the Scott defense, only Henry sided with the Union during the Civil War. It is unclear when he changed his position on slave-holding—whether it was before the Dred Scott decade or during—but it definitely preceded the Civil War. Susan and Nellie, at school in New York, were worried about national events and their family back home. The Southern girls had all left school, and by the end of June, 1861, Miss Haines closed her school and sent the rest of the pupils home. Arriving at Old Southampton, the girls found a large United States flag flying on the roof.

Susan, almost twenty, had become an attractive and popular young woman with blue eyes, light-brown hair, and a petite "graceful figure." She was a frequent guest at parties held at the nearby Jefferson Barracks. The military installation sat on 1,700 acres acquired from the Village of Carondelet. In addition to its importance as a munitions depot and military hospital, it was a prime post for basic training. Thousands of young men moved in and out of the post, but while they were there, they found time for dancing and fun. At one officers' dance, Susan met an upcoming young colonel, William Coyle. Henry had higher aspirations for his daughter, and he and Minerva tried to discourage the friendship, even suggesting that Colonel Coyle had serious health problems. Undeterred, Susan continued to correspond with William when war duties took him out of the area.

Her father, meanwhile, had been elected to the US Congress and was spending a lot of time in Washington, DC. He sent money home so

Susan could travel to Washington. She spent several months there, and Henry did all he could to promote matches between his daughter and candidates he considered more suitable than her colonel.

Upon her return to St. Louis, Susan continued to write to William—in spite of her mother's scolding and her father's insistence that she report to him all her correspondence with the young man. It seemed providential to the parents when Colonel Coyle was relieved of duty for "medical reasons" and moved to Kentucky, where he was appointed to the position of judge advocate. There is no evidence that Susan suspected her father's political connections had anything to do with the move—and perhaps they didn't. Apparently, this development did put an end to the association. Although Susan had many friends over the years, none was as special as Colonel William Coyle and she never married.

Henry Blow retired from the Congress in 1867. Two years later, President Grant, a personal friend, appointed him minister to Brazil. Blow and his family were feted at what was described in the invitation as a "grand banquet" before their departure.

Susan, with her agile mind, quickly learned Portuguese, the language of Brazil, and served as her father's secretary. His mission was to establish trade ties in Brazil in order to help balance the US trade deficit. During the Civil War, all activities were geared toward the conflict, leaving the US behind other countries in exporting goods. Henry wrote to Washington, "Our problem is to prepare for selling to Brazil everything she requires from abroad as cheap or cheaper than other nations and especially those articles we are so well-fitted to produce." Susan not only helped with translation but also prepared communiqués to Washington.

It wasn't all work, however. The country was beautiful with miles of seashore on the Atlantic Ocean, and the diplomatic community provided a round of social activities. In these circles Susan's sister Nellie met the love of her life, Count Theodor Smirnoff, a diplomat attached to the Russian Embassy. Before he returned to Russia, he invited the entire Blow family to visit him and promised them a grand tour of Europe.

After Henry's two-year assignment in Brazil, the family decided to accept the invitation. Susan had always been interested in education and was particularly intrigued with the concepts of Friedrich Froebel in Germany. She took the opportunity on the trip to visit a number of kindergartens, observing and taking copious notes.

Froebel, who had died in 1852, had opened his first kindergarten in 1837, although the designation "kindergarten" wasn't applied until 1840. The term referred to both a physical garden where children could observe nature and a educational garden where children could grow through structured activities. Froebel divided activities into "gifts and occupations" and "games of social cooperation and control." Gifts and occupations activities were designed using specific materials, including blocks, balls, paper, clay, and other objects. Games included dramatic play, games of skill, and songs. While in Germany, Susan purchased several of Froebel's prescribed objects.

Upon arrival at home, she began planning her own kindergarten. Henry offered to finance it, but she wanted to see the program available to all children. There were several private kindergartens back East, but Susan hoped to see the program offered through the public schools. She found an able ally—William Torrey Harris—the St. Louis superintendent of schools.

Harris was familiar with the kindergarten movement and appointed a committee to determine the feasibility of adding the program. The committee's findings were favorable, and the school board approved plans for a kindergarten with Susan as director.

Before undertaking the task, Susan asked for more time for training. She returned to New York to Miss Haines' school, where Maria Boelté had established a kindergarten. Boelté had studied with Luise Froebel, Friedrich's widow, in her home country, Germany. Susan couldn't have had a better tutor. and upon completion of the course, she was ready to meet her first class.

The new Des Peres School had been completed while she was in New York, and she actually missed the first few days of classes, which were conducted by her first assistant and two volunteers. Susan arrived several days later to discover the classroom had been designed in a traditional manner, and she soon transformed it, to the amazement of the children. One of her first pupils later wrote, "This was a great step forward for in those days the schoolroom was the barest of the bare."

The children loved kindergarten and they loved "Miss Susie." One of her students remembered, "One day I was suddenly seized with a fit of homesickness and Miss Susie in her gentle, loving fashion took me on her lap and told me a little story about two small buckets, one behind each eye, that turned over and spilled out the water for tears when I wanted to cry. I afterwards told this to many of my own little scholars."

Susan's care of her students extended outside of school hours, too. The same former student described a party Susie gave for the class, "[T]he ice cream was frozen like a big white hen and lots of little yellow chickens. When I was given a little chicken my delight was so great that I carried it around the house until it melted all over my blue sash but I could not be persuaded to give it up until Miss Susie herself took me to her room and induced me to let her wash off what was left of the ice cream."

By the end of the year, the program was ready for evaluation. The school board report concluded:

> *The formation of habits of cleanliness and politeness is marked and successful but the development of the intellect in making quantitative and mathematical combinations is more surprising. On an intellectual level, Harris's goal for the program was to serve as a civilizing agent. Susan's goals included personal development leading to productive individuals with heightened*

intellectual and moral awareness. Susan put aside philosophical terminology in succinctly describing the success of the program, "The strongest claim is the happiness it produces.

Susan continued to teach, with no pay—children in the morning and classes to train teachers and assistants in the afternoon. For the 1874 term, almost all the children returned and there was a waiting list for the class. A second kindergarten room was added mid-year. By 1876, the St. Louis school system had twelve kindergarten classes.

That was the year of the Philadelphia Centennial Exposition to celebrate the nation's one-hundredth birthday. In conjunction with the Women's Pavilion, a Kindergarten Cottage was erected. Susan was instrumental in the design and outfitting of the model classroom, which was housed in its own small building. Visitors could watch local orphans being taught by the Froebel method and purchase Froebel materials. One of the visitors who purchased blocks for her little boy was Anna Lloyd Jones Wright. Her son Frank would become one of America's greatest architects. The St. Louis public schools were recognized by the Centennial Commission with an award of excellence, and Susan was given an award for "service to education."

St. Louis had forty-one kindergarten classes by 1878, and in 1880, the board voted to open classes in every white school in the district as soon as space was available. In 1883, the program was added to the black schools.

Susan continued to work, unpaid, for the St. Louis schools until 1884, and she left the city four years later. She continued teaching teachers and lecturing, and she wrote five books between 1890 and 1899, one a study of Dante, the other four about aspects of education and Froebel's methods.

In 1898, she began teaching at the Teachers' College at Columbia University, where she taught for several years. However, winds of change were sweeping through the kindergarten. Many people felt the Froebel method was too rigid; Susan did not. It was a battle she could not win, and she left the school. She continued to lecture around the country until three weeks before her death on March 26, 1916. She was seventy-two years old.

Friedrich Froebel's motto had been "Let us live for the children." That message was displayed on the wall of Susan Elizabeth Blow's first kindergarten, and it was the motto by which she lived.

CATHY WILLIAMS

(1844–?)
BUFFALO SOLDIER

S he seemed to have nothing going for her. She was a woman, she was black, and she was a slave. She probably couldn't read or write. She was barely even a footnote in history, but she was remarkable.

Her name was Cathy Williams. Her last name was probably the same as one of her mother's owners. She was born in 1844, and died sometime between 1892 and 1900; in between her birth and her death, she lived an amazing life. Yet, we know almost nothing about her. Most of her personal information comes from an article in the *St. Louis Daily Times* published January 2, 1876.

In the *Times* article, Cathy reported, "My father was a free man, but my mother a slave, belonging to William Johnson, a wealthy farmer who lived at the time I was born near Independence, Jackson County, Missouri."

Unlike the large cotton plantation owners of the South, the slave owners in Missouri were often small farmers, the Johnsons among them. The land around Independence consisted of rolling terrain and fertile soil. Independence itself was a bustling town—the northern terminus of the Santa Fe Trail, and the town grew prosperous supplying goods and services to pioneers. In May, 1845, one thousand wagons left Independence, gathering on Liberty Street to begin the 1,200-mile trek.

Another activity that took place on Liberty Street was the local slave auction. Many Missourians came from Southern states and had slaves, and they wanted to keep them. In 1820, an agreement called the Missouri Compromise allowed Missouri to enter the Union as a slave state. The agreement also stipulated that, in the future, slavery would be abolished in any part of the Louisiana Purchase north of the southern border of

Cathy Williams Printed and used with the permission of the Buffalo Soldiers Educational and Historical Committee and William Jennings (artist)

Missouri. This arrangement held until 1854, when passage of the Kansas-Nebraska Act enabled voters in those territories to decide whether slavery would be allowed within their boundaries. Because of this, the Kansas-Missouri border became a war zone well before the beginning of the Civil War, and Independence was in the middle of the fight.

The Johnsons left Jackson County in 1850, moving near Jefferson City in Cole County in the middle of the state. Cathy was old enough to do simple chores in the house, perhaps setting the table or making beds. She probably did some field chores, too; during harvest, it was common for everyone to pitch in. Cathy certainly didn't go to school. It was against the law to teach a slave to read or write, and anyone caught teaching these skills to a slave could be fined and thrown in jail.

Sometime between 1850 and 1860, Cathy's master died. Apparently, Mrs. Johnson was able to continue to run the farm and keep the slaves. In the meantime, the political situation in the state was becoming more rancorous. With the Kansas-Nebraska Act in place, Missouri slave-holders were anxious for their neighbor to the west—Kansas Territory—to be a slave state, too. Missourians crossed the border to push their position, while abolitionists crowded into the territory to discourage the extension of slavery.

Things were tense elsewhere, also. Following the election of President Lincoln in 1860, seven states seceded from the Union. In April, 1861, Confederate forces fired on and captured Fort Sumter, a federal installation in the Charleston, South Carolina, harbor.

The governor of Missouri was pro-slavery and wanted the state to secede. A convention to decide the issue was called, and the vote went to the anti-secession faction. The unhappy governor, Claiborne Jackson, not only refused to send troops to fight for the Union, he also called for volunteers to join the state militia to fight for the Confederacy.

After Governor Jackson refused to send men to support the Union, he and the leader of the Missouri militia, General Sterling Price (a former governor of Missouri), and General Nathaniel Lyon (commander of the US arsenal near St. Louis) met to try to reach a peaceful solution. They failed. On June 11, 1861, the meeting broke up with General Lyon declaring, "This means war. In an hour one of my officers will call for you and conduct you out of my lines."

By mid-June Lyon's army had chased Jackson halfway across the state and captured Jefferson City. Unready for battle, the governor and militia deserted the capital leaving it in Union hands. The army considered slaves contraband of war and took them to serve with the moving troops. Black men couldn't enlist in the army but undoubtedly fought side-by-side with the regular soldiers.

Cathy was in a precarious position, with no home and no occupation in the midst of pro-slavery territory. The Union army offered food and shelter. Cathy was in legal limbo—technically no longer a slave but not exactly free. She described this period of her life to the *Times* reporter, ". . . when the war broke out and the United States soldiers came to Jefferson City they took me and other colored folks with them to Little Rock. Colonel Benton of the Thirteenth Army Corps was the officer that carried us off. I did not want to go. He wanted me to cook for the officers, but I had always been a house girl and did not know how to cook."

Cathy was like a leaf in a whirlwind. She went where the Eighth Regiment Infantry went. She spent several months encamped in an earthworks fortification near Otterville before heading south toward Springfield. The regiment was involved in several skirmishes on the trip.

As difficult as Cathy's life as a slave had been, this was worse. The terrain was rough and the weather rougher. Because she couldn't cook, Cathy served as a laundress. Her clothes were inadequate for the trip, and she had to carry her laundry supplies and sleep on the ground like the soldiers.

In March, the Eighth was involved in the Battle of Pea Ridge— a two-day encounter with many casualties and almost one thousand Union soldiers wounded. Cathy likely was pressed into service as a nurse. The victory secured Missouri for the Union and opened Arkansas for the Union forces.

As the Union army rolled through Arkansas, more blacks joined the march. The Eighth continued across the state to the Mississippi. Cathy had walked more than five hundred miles—and wasn't finished. Next, she was sent to Little Rock, where she learned to cook. Then the Eighth went on to Vicksburg.

When she was reunited with the Indiana troops, she went with the men through Louisiana and down into east Texas, near the Aransas Pass. The group left Texas to go to New Orleans, then up the Mississippi River. For the first time on her journey, Cathy didn't have to walk—the Eighth went by steamboat.

Ultimately, they headed east and Cathy was transferred from the Eighth. Cathy reported, "Finally I was sent to Washington City and at the time General Sheridan made his raids in the Shenandoah valley I was cook and washwoman for his staff."

Imagine the action that went on around this young black woman. A number of battles had been fought in the Shenandoah Valley before General Philip Sheridan was made commander of the Union forces in what became the Army of the Shenandoah. In a series of battles, success switched back and forth between the conflicting armies. By late September, 1864, the Union seemed to have the upper hand as Sheridan moved across the land—burning farms, fields, and factories—to starve the Confederates of food and supplies.

Things came to a head in mid-October when the Confederate soldiers overran the Union headquarters, scattering troops in a scramble to save themselves. Sheridan managed to regroup and counterattack, defeating the rebels. Cathy, in her position serving the general and his retinue, was in the midst of the melee.

Following this period, Cathy was transferred back to the Eighth Indiana, following them to Baltimore and then south to Savannah. General

William Tecumseh Sherman, following his capture of Atlanta, had made his "March to the Sea," taking the city of Savannah on December 21, 1864. The Eighth arrived soon after and remained in Savannah as part of an occupying force until the end of the war. Members of the Eighth Regiment Infantry were released from service on August 28, 1865. After returning to Indiana, the troops were mustered out in September.

Cathy was truly free after years of slavery and four years with the army. It must have been frightening; her whole life until that time had been controlled by others. She made her way back to St. Louis, where she found work, probably as a laundress or cook. Living in the vicinity of Jefferson Barracks, she was aware of what was happening there. The war was over, but threats to the nation persisted—unease in relations with Mexico and tensions between Native Americans and settlers who were pouring into the western territories.

Following the issuance of Lincoln's Emancipation Proclamation, Negroes were, for the first time, allowed to enlist in the regular army. Jefferson Barracks was a major recruitment center.

Life was hard, and although Cathy was used to that, it was even more difficult for a single woman to support herself in those days. Cathy must have thought long and hard before taking her next step. Disguising herself as a man, she marched up to Jefferson Barracks and presented herself for enlistment in the army.

Cathy later showed the *Times* reporter her military papers and said, "You will see by this paper that on the 15th day of November, 1866, I enlisted in the United States army at St. Louis, in the Thirty-eighth United States Infantry, company A., Capt. Charles E. Clarke commanding."

Cathy was tall and strong from a life of hard work. She told the recruiter her name was William Cathy, which he spelled "Cathey," and she, not being able to write, made an X on the line. Her enlistment physical must have been a mere formality, because the doctor declared her fit for service, missing the fact that "William" was a woman.

Her true identity was known by only two other people. "The regiment I joined wore the Zouave uniform and only two persons, a cousin and a particular friend, members of the regiment, knew that I was a woman. They never 'blowed' on me. They were partly the cause of my joining the army. Another reason was I wanted to make my own living and not be dependent on relations or friends," Cathy said later.

Cathy was now part of one of a number of new regiments created that year. These included six black regiments—two cavalry and four infantry—which would become known as Buffalo Soldiers.

In the spring of 1867, Cathy came down with smallpox and was sent to a hospital in East St. Louis. Again, the doctors seemed to miss a basic fact about their patient. While she was hospitalized, her company, along with Company B, began a move to the west. Cathy caught up with them later that spring at Fort Riley in Kansas. By April 10, Cathy was back in the hospital—this time with the "itch," a condition caused by minute parasites burrowing into her skin. Although hospitalized for over a month, she still managed to maintain her disguise!

Disease seemed to be a major part of life in the late 1800s. Cholera, an intestinal disease caused by eating or drinking contaminated food or water, was a major killer. Cathy and her regiment marched from Ft. Riley about eighty-five miles to Fort Harker. While there, cholera broke out. Though the disease was probably being spread by immigrants coming through on wagon trains, rumor blamed the black soldiers as the source of the epidemic. Rather than the cause, the soldiers of the Thirty-Eighth were victims, with many of the men succumbing to the ailment. Before the epidemic abated, over thirty soldiers had died from the disease.

In the meantime, the Plains Indians, reacting to the influx of pioneers and General Sheridan's war on both the Native Americans and the buffalo, which were crucial to their way of life, were raiding and retaliating wherever they could. In late June, the men of the Thirty-Eighth Infantry were ordered to report to Fort Union in New Mexico, about five hundred miles southwest. Cathy and her companions spent only a couple of weeks at Fort Union before they were ordered to Fort Cummings—a march of over 350 miles.

So far, the soldiers of Company A had spent most of their military lives moving from one post to the next. They had seen little action, and due to new treaties with the Plains tribes, the frontier was less dangerous.

However, the trip to Fort Cummings had its own hazards. The landscape was arid and the nights were chilly. The march was difficult, the rations short, and failing to reach a good crossing of the Rio Grande, the soldiers were forced to swim across the river.

Located in southwest New Mexico Territory, Fort Cummings was in the very heart of Apache territory. The Apaches in this part of the country were among the last of the tribes to give up their fight for their way of life, their territory, and their freedom. They were notorious for their hit-and-run attacks, against which infantry troops were almost useless.

In the desert landscape wood was scarce, and the soldiers' duties included gathering firewood for the fort. The fort had been in existence for several years, so all the nearby kindling had been exhausted, which meant soldiers had to venture farther away from the safety of the walled fort. This and other tension-filled tasks lowered the morale of the troops. The black soldiers also felt they were assigned the most difficult, dangerous, and dirty duties.

In this charged atmosphere, all it would take to spark a confrontation was a relatively minor incident—and that happened. One of the officers, Second Lieutenant Henry Leggett, was particularly unpopular with the men of Company A. Early in December, he accused a black woman, a civilian working at the fort as his maid, of stealing money. The maid was searched, and although no money was found, she was banished from the fort. The black soldiers were incensed by her treatment, and their anger escalated into a situation that ended in mutiny. A number of the Buffalo Soldiers were arrested and faced court martial.

Cathy had to have been aware of what had transpired and was surely sympathetic to the maid, having once been a civilian traveling with the army herself. It was, however, necessary for her to stay out of trouble and avoid special notice. She later told the *Times* reporter, "I was a good soldier . . . was never put in the guard house, no bayonet was ever put to my back. I carried my musket and did guard and other duties while in the army, but finally I got tired and wanted to get off."

If Cathy was discouraged by the treatment she and her fellow Buffalo Soldiers received at the fort, the campaign that began January 1, 1868, certainly didn't mitigate her dissatisfaction. Troops from three forts—Cummings, Bayard, and Craig—were supposed to meet and attack an Apache village that was suspected of being a center for raiding forays. Typically, the mounted units were used for chasing the Indians, but because the village was too far from the forts, the terrain too rough, and water too scarce for the animals, the infantry got the assignment.

A small band of twenty-five soldiers, including Cathy, headed out from the fort. The weather was cold and their uniforms were flimsy. They had to trek through several creeks, soaking their socks and shoes. They crossed miles of rough territory, the only sounds the shuffle of their feet and the occasional cry of a circling hawk, knowing that at any moment they could walk into an ambush because they had no cavalry scout to reconnoiter the areas into which they marched. There was nowhere to hide or to shelter from the cold, and they couldn't build a fire because the smoke would signal their location.

They expected to rendezvous with the troops from the other forts. No reinforcements arrived. Finally, their commanding officer made the difficult decision to retreat. The only positive outcome of the whole miserable expedition was that it proved once more that the Buffalo Soldiers performed admirably under difficult conditions. For Cathy the mission resulted in two more hospital stays—again, with her secret going undetected.

In June, Company A set out again, this time reporting to Fort Bayard, northwest of Fort Cummings. Like Cummings, the fort was a target of Apache raids. It was also notable for its lack of amenities. The structures were crude and accommodations uncomfortable.

When it became obvious that General Sheridan was planning another major expedition to wipe out the recalcitrant Indians, Cathy had had enough. She was tired, and her body had taken a beating over the two years she'd spent with the infantry. The racial tensions and obvious discrimination in her last postings no doubt contributed to her decision, as well. So, in the fall of 1868, Cathy again entered the infirmary—this time leaving behind all the tricks and subterfuges that had allowed her to escape discovery in the past. As she told the St. Louis writer, "The post surgeon found out I was a woman and I got my discharge."

There was, of course, more to it than that. As word spread around the camp, her long-time companions turned on her, probably chagrined at having been so thoroughly duped. Even Captain Clarke, who never complained about her during her service, chimed in with criticism. In the newspaper interview Cathy downplayed the event just as she'd downplayed the rest of her life. "The men wanted to get rid of me after they found out I was a woman. Some of them acted real bad to me."

For the second time in her life, Cathy Williams was completely free. She had gone from being a slave to being swept up by the Union army during the Civil War. She had served the army as a civilian for almost four years and as a soldier for two years. Now, at only twenty-four years old, she was on her own again.

Cathy returned to the Fort Union area and found work as a cook for an army officer and his family. She lived in several places in northeast New Mexico and southeastern Colorado, finding employment cooking and laundering. Even though the jobs were menial, Cathy was a hard worker and managed to save some money.

Eight years later, in 1878, she was living in Trinidad, Colorado, where the *St. Louis Daily Times* reporter found her. She was living in her own home, a small adobe structure, sparsely furnished but "neat and tidy." She told the reporter, "After leaving the army I went to Pueblo, Colorado, where I made money by cooking and washing. I got married while there, but my husband was no account. He stole my watch and chain, a hundred dollars in money and my team of horses and wagon. I had him arrested and put in jail."

She went on to talk about the town. "I like this town. I know all the good people here and I expect to get rich yet. . . . You see I've got a good sewing machine and I get washing to do and clothes to make. I want to get along and not be a burden to my friends or relatives."

Facts about the rest of Cathy's life are as sparse as those of her early life. She had more health problems. At some point, all of her toes were amputated and she was no longer able to work. She applied for a soldier's disability pension but was denied. She disappears from official records after 1892 and is absent from the 1900 census, indicating she probably died during that period. Cathy Williams is buried in an unmarked grave.

Cathy Williams lived an unusual and independent life. That she—illiterate, black, and a woman—was so resourceful in creating a life for herself says a great deal about her determination and strength. She walked thousands of miles in her lifetime, and she charted her own course to freedom.

Virginia Alice Cottey Stockard

—•◦•—

(1848–1940)

ARCHITECT OF AN INSTITUTION

The two women must have felt daunted as they entered the room full of men. They had such big plans. In 1883, women could teach school—but build one? They had prepared diligently, making contacts in several towns to gauge community interest in an institution of education for girls and young women. Several places had expressed interest, but Nevada, Missouri, seemed just right to Alice Cottey and her younger sister, Dora. Letters had been exchanged, but now, meeting face-to-face, Alice had to communicate her ideas to this audience—and convince them to invest in her vision.

Alice had done her homework. She had already consulted an architect and sent preliminary plans to Nevada. A contractor had given her estimates of building costs. Upon arrival in town, she and Dora had been taken to see several possible building sites.

Now she addressed the committee, saying, "If you will purchase the grounds for the college and donate them to me . . . I will proceed at once to erect a three-story building sufficient to accommodate eighty students and I will add to this building as the need arises." She continued, "We propose to inaugurate a thorough course of study, embracing all the branches of a young ladies' college curriculum."

The men were impressed with her businesslike approach and the forethought she had given the project. A number of them expressed support. The women were hopeful but knew the job was not finished. After they left Nevada to return home, a meeting of the town would determine

Virginia Alice Cottey Stockard Courtesy of Cottey College

the fate of the school. How relieved they were when, a few days later, they received a telegram from the committee saying that a deal had been struck for the land and funds were coming in for payment. Alice Cottey had a commitment, a six-acre corn field, and a big job ahead of her.

Virginia Alice Cottey, always known as Alice, was the fifth child born to Sarah Elizabeth Eads and Ira Day Cottey. The first two children died before Alice was born. Her mother, father, and brothers William and Lewis (Lou) were living in a small log cabin on Bee Ridge, nine miles southeast of Edina, Missouri.

Alice was born on March 27, 1848. Two years later, Mary Matilda was born. The little cabin was getting crowded, so Ira sold his farm and bought another place nearby. A two-story, frame house with gingerbread trim on the eaves and a big front porch went with the property—just right for the expanding family, which kept on growing. Mary was followed by Ann, Miriam, Ira, Ella, and finally, Kate, in 1863. Father Cottey had to add on to the house twice.

During these years, the Civil War brought turmoil to Missouri. The Cotteys didn't have slaves, nor did they advocate secession; their sympathies, however, were with the South. Although Missouri had no big-name battles like Manassas or Shiloh, a lot of action took place in the state—from Wilson's Creek in the southwest and Westport in the northwest. In all, Missouri had about four hundred military encounters, many of which were guerrilla actions by unauthorized groups.

Even in northeast Missouri, where the Cotteys lived, people were in constant fear from actions on both sides of the dispute. The Cottey children's most vivid memory of the conflict was perhaps of the time a group of Union soldiers came to the house demanding to be fed. Mother Cottey and the older girls quickly prepared a meal for the men and were relieved when the group departed. As the men rode off, the family dog chased behind them, barking. One of the soldiers pulled his gun and shot the pet—a traumatic ending to a dramatic encounter.

With the ending of the war, Sarah and Ira could again plan for the future. They were concerned over their children's lack of education. It's uncertain how much formal schooling they had received at this point. Local schools, if they existed, provided only minimal education, and teachers were often little ahead of their students. Will was already twenty-one, Lou nineteen, and Alice seventeen. Will's help was invaluable on the farm, but it was decided Lou would go to a private school in Palmyra—about fifty miles away on today's modern roads, a long trip by horseback or wagon.

No schools for girls were available nearby, and most people thought girls didn't need an education, anyway. All they needed to do was learn to cook, sew, and keep house. The Cotteys had always valued education, and their children read voraciously. Alice had already read the Bible, *The Pilgrim's Progress,* and the works of Shakespeare plus any books she'd been able to borrow from neighbors. When Lou came home for the summer, Alice borrowed some of his books and even taught herself Latin.

As she studied on her own, she longed for a place where girls could be taught the same subjects as boys. As a devout Methodist, she must have prayed for such a place—and she must have been surprised when she received a Catholic answer. The Sisters of Loretto had arrived in Edina and opened St. Joseph's Academy for girls.

Because of the distance she would have to go as a boarding student. Leaving home was difficult, but it was the opportunity she'd been hoping for. It was 1866, and Alice, at eighteen, was ready and eager for more education. The school taught only to the tenth grade, and by the end of the year, Alice had easily mastered everything the nuns had to teach her.

The following fall she left for Newark to attend a private high school. Even with courses in Latin and mathematics, Alice sailed through the curriculum. At the close of the term, she accepted her first teaching position in one of the schools in her home county, Knox County.

At this time, all that was necessary to teach was a certificate obtained by taking a test. Many teachers had little education themselves, and some had gotten jobs through political contacts. Alice's pupils were lucky because she not only had a better education than most teachers but she also was kind and patient with her students.

Her little sister, Dora, was not so fortunate. The teacher at the Bee Ridge School terrified and bullied the children. When Alice came home for the summer, she discovered that her little brother and sisters were woefully behind in some subjects. To help them catch up, she set up her own little school—with classes sometimes held on the big porch or under a shady tree. Neighbors who heard what she was doing quickly approached her to teach their children, too. In a few weeks that summer, the children learned more than in the entire past term.

Meanwhile, Lou had graduated from college, studied law, and been admitted to the bar. With his help, Alice moved to Richmond College to teach. This job lasted two years, until Lou, who had been elected superintendent of Knox County District Schools, asked her to take the Bee Ridge School.

By the late 1870s, Alice was teaching at the Central Female College in Lexington, Missouri. Dora, after graduating there, also joined the faculty. In her spare time, Alice took classes at the college and became involved in the Women's Missionary Society. In 1880, Dora moved to Texas to teach at the Dallas Female College.

Father Cottey died in the spring of 1883. While Alice was home that summer, she became reacquainted with a book that had been a favorite of hers years before—*The Power of Christian Benevolence, Illustrated in the Life and Letters of Mary Lyon.* Mary Lyon was the founder of Mt. Holyoke Female Seminary in South Hadley, Massachusetts, in 1837. Back at Central, Alice reread the book, paying close attention to the details of founding the seminary. She evaluated each step, thinking, *If I were going to have my own school, would this work for me?* She liked the ideas of affordability and accessibility coupled with entrance exams to determine placement. She approved of providing a broad curriculum, stressing religion, and the possibilities of missionary work. Teaching women to be good teachers was another positive goal. Mary's efforts to finance her school demonstrated the practical difficulties she would face. But she wasn't so sure about Mary Lyon's view of the incompatibility of marriage and having a school.

With her sister Dora, Alice shared her fantasy of having her own school. Dora pointed out that Alice was thirty-five—high time to stop dreaming and start working toward her goal. Of course, money was a problem. But Dora had the answer to that, too. She and their sister Mary together had two thousand dollars, which combined with money Alice had saved, Dora figured, should be enough to get the project off the ground.

Alice began writing letters to Southern Methodist ministers in Missouri, inquiring about possible locations for a school for girls. Dora, back in Texas, wrote letters in that state. Several locations responded, but correspondence with Reverend W. T. McClure in Nevada was particularly promising. Both Dora and Alice hoped the school would be located in their home state.

After the visit to Nevada, plans and progress proceeded with surprising speed. Ground-breaking took place on March 8, 1884. As soon as her teaching term at Central ended, Alice moved to Nevada to oversee the work. The building contractor was an old hand at construction, but working for a woman was a new experience. Apparently, the hardest part of his job was cleaning up his language for the lady boss.

The sisters' money helped start the project, but Alice knew they needed more funds to get the school going. Her primary method of raising funds for the school was to sell scholarships. The school was organized into three classifications: primary with five levels, intermediate and collegiate with three levels each. Tuition fees were determined based on the educational level of the student. A year's tuition for a non-boarding student at the college level cost forty dollars. Purchasing an eighty-dollar transferable scholarship guaranteed the donor three years' tuition. The offer was good for a limited time, making it possible to secure funds as quickly as possible.

The school opened on September 8, 1884, less than a year after the first meeting with the committee in Nevada. There were twenty-eight students, twelve of whom were boarders. The faculty consisted of Alice, "principal and teacher of languages and ethics"; her sister Dora, "teacher of mathematics, elocution and calisthenics"; her sister Mary, "teacher of painting, drawing, and principal of the primary department"; and Miss Olive N. Harrison, "instructor of music, both vocal and instrumental." Alice's dream had become reality.

The school was first called Vernon Seminary after the county where it was located. From the beginning, however, townspeople referred to it as "the Cottey sisters' school," and eventually, "Cottey College." In 1887, after Alice modestly acquiesced, the state officially chartered the school as Cottey College.

The school continued to grow. Fund-raising seemed a never-ending task, and inevitably, change came to the institution. Dora married in 1888 and moved to Lexington, where her husband and original supporter, the Reverend W. T. McClure, held a pastorate. A replacement was found for Dora, and their youngest sister, Kate, came to teach typing and shorthand and to help with administrative duties.

Several years earlier, a new student had come to Cottey—little Katie Stockard. Katie's mother had died, leaving her father with two boys and Katie. Alice took the little girl under her wing. It was difficult for Mr. Stockard to work and care for the boys, so a year later John and George came to live at the school. Mr. Stockard visited as often as he could.

Alice had had suitors before, but she'd never met a man for whom she was willing to give up her idea of a school. By the age of forty, the possibility of marriage and a family seemed remote. She had, however, become a surrogate mother to the three Stockard children and already grown very fond of lively Katie with her musical ability, studious John, and helpful, handy George.

Mr. Stockard might not have been the man of Alice's dreams, but she enjoyed his good humor and loved his children. He was also a Methodist, even though he wasn't particularly religious. On his part, Mr. Stockard could not have found anyone who would care more lovingly for his children—and he knew it. Alice was also an attractive, intelligent woman of whom he had become very fond. He proposed, and Alice, after much consideration, accepted.

Although the Stockard children and Alice's family knew of the engagement, it did not become public knowledge until the afternoon of March 6, 1890. Alice announced to the girls in study hall that tea, crackers, and sardines would be served at five o'clock. They must have been surprised at this unusual arrangement—even more so when Alice continued: "At eight I want you to come to the parlor for my wedding. There will be dinner afterward." So it was that Virginia Alice Cottey became Virginia Alice Cottey Stockard.

Sam Stockard turned out to be a good listening ear for Alice and also took over some of the burden of recruiting students from her. Their marriage was not to last long, however. After only six years, while away on a business trip, Sam Stockard suffered a heart attack and died. While their marriage might have been one of convenience more so than romance, it was a truly caring relationship, and Alice mourned and missed Sam deeply.

Through the years, Alice devoted herself single-mindedly to the school, but she was smart enough and unselfish enough to realize it would not be hers forever. In 1892, she organized an advisory board to help her. She was also on the lookout for an entity that would guarantee the perpetuation of the school. In 1922, she turned over the presidency to Doctor J. C. Harmon, hoping that a male president would build confidence. Doctor Harmon, however, resigned after only two years, and Alice again took the leadership of the college.

In 1924, a local chapter of PEO (Philanthropic Educational Organization), a national organization founded in 1869 to promote educational opportunities for women, held an event at the school to raise money for the PEO educational fund. It was the first association of many between the organization and the college. Alice formally joined the group two years later.

The organization's ideals and Alice's ideals meshed beautifully. and in 1927, she offered the college to PEO at their national convention in Oklahoma City. It was a match made in heaven. That same year she was named Missouri's Woman of the Year.

Alice continued to serve as president of Cottey College until 1929. She remained close to the school, still attending chapel services, often giving the Bible reading, and leading prayers for a number of years.

The school she had founded had grown from one small building on a bare field to a number of buildings on a beautiful, tree-shaded campus. She oversaw the intellectual and spiritual growth of thousands of young women. If ever anyone could claim the scripture, "I have fought the good fight, I have finished the race, I have kept the faith," it was Virginia Alice Cottey Stockard. She died on July 16, 1940, at the age of ninety-two. The college she founded stands today as a testament to her commitment to the education of young women.

KATE CHOPIN

(1850–1904)
AUTHOR AHEAD OF HER TIME

K ate Chopin, nurtured by a family of strong women, was a woman of strong opinions. She gained fame—and some notoriety—with her writing skills and her willingness to tackle controversial subjects. Her stories are full of characters based on people she knew and on situations in which she was a participant or a likely observer. For some years following her death, she and her works were relegated to obscurity. Today, however, her writings are taught in universities, and she is widely regarded as an important American author.

Kate was born in St. Louis in 1850—an exciting time and place. What had been a sleepy French village in 1803 when the Louisiana Purchase was signed had become a busy river town and an important outfitting stop for travelers heading west to the Santa Fe, Oregon, and California Trails. The town's population had skyrocketed, and its port was second in size only to New York City's.

In addition to the original French inhabitants and the Americans moving west, forty-three percent of the residents were immigrants from Ireland and Germany. Kate's family was the perfect example of St. Louis diversity, with her mother, Eliza, of French extraction and her father, Thomas, an Irish immigrant.

Prior to marrying Eliza, Thomas O'Flaherty had settled in St. Louis, built a business, established a reputation as a respected businessman, and married the daughter of a French-Canadian merchant. The couple had a son, George, and were expecting another child. Unfortunately, both mother and child died in childbirth.

Kate Chopin Courtesy of the Missouri Historical Museum, St. Louis

Eliza Faris was the oldest child of seven children. Her father had deserted her mother, leaving her with a large family and little money. Although Eliza's mother came from a well-established French family, the Charlevilles, she received no help from them because her father disapproved of her marriage.

Thomas had a young son and needed a wife, preferably one from a respectable family with St. Louis connections. Eliza's mother needed a way out of her financial predicament. So sixteen-year-old Eliza married thirty-nine-year-old Thomas; in exchange, Thomas paid the family's debts and sent Eliza's brothers and sisters to school. Four years later, the couple had a son, Tom, and two years after that, Catherine O'Flaherty was born.

Known as Kate, Catherine was a determined little girl with a mind of her own. She had a keen interest in what went on in the wider world, and she was curious about what her father did after he left the house in the morning. At a time when children were to be seen and not heard, she apparently was so persistent that one day he took her with him. His business was located on the riverfront. All the sights, smells, and sounds of the riverfront filled the air—the smoke from the steamboats, the odor of the river, the shouts of the workers. Perhaps this experience gave Kate her first inkling of the sheltered life that she and women in general led during that time.

By 1855, St. Louis was on the move. The first segment of the first railroad designed to stretch from St. Louis to the West Coast had been completed, running 125 miles to Jefferson City, the state capital. Six hundred citizens—including a group of St. Louis dignitaries, among them Thomas O'Flaherty—boarded the train for the first trip out of St. Louis. As the train crossed over the Gasconade River, the bridge collapsed, dumping the locomotive and all but one of the cars into the river. Miraculously, fewer than forty people were killed. That miracle did not include Thomas O'Flaherty.

The O'Flaherty household was large and included Kate's grand-mother, aunts, uncles, great-grandmother, and servants. Five-year-old Kate had been at boarding school when the accident that took her father's life occurred. Her mother immediately brought her home, and she didn't return to school for two years. During that time her great-grandmother, Victoire Charleville, became her most important mentor.

Madame Charleville tutored young Kate in French and piano. She also shared with her St. Louis history, spiced with stories of historic figures—the kinds of stories textbooks didn't include. Many of the stories featured strong women, including Madame Charleville's own mother, Victoire Verdon, who had emigrated to the United States from France. Madame Verdon walked away from a contentious marriage, and athough illiterate, she started a business trading notions (pins, needles, buttons, ribbons, etc.) in little towns along the river. Before her death, she had built her enterprise into a company involving a number of trading vessels.

Madame Charleville was both pragmatic and practical in her outlook, and she shared her wisdom with her great-granddaughter. She considered marriage more of a business arrangement than a romantic pairing.

In a household of single women, Kate saw independent women in control of their own affairs—observations that became ingrained in her own character.

When she was seven, Kate went back to the Academy of the Sacred Heart. There, she made friends with another girl, Kitty Garesché, who would be her best friend for the next six years. The girls went to school together and played together. They loved ice-skating in the winter and climbing trees in the summer. But most of all, they loved reading.

While Kate and Kitty played, events around them were becom-ing ominous. Many St. Louisans had slaves, including the O'Flahertys, but many adamant abolitionists also lived in the town. While Missouri never seceded from the Union, the entire state was conflicted about the issue. With the firing on Fort Sumter in April 1861, the reality of war came to the city.

In May, Union soldiers broke up an assembly of the Southern-sympathizing Missouri militia. Shots were fired and people were killed. A Union prison was established close to the O'Flaherty home, and the newly appointed commander of the Army of the West, John C. Fremont, took up residence in a mansion just a few doors from Kate's house. Union troops were everywhere, and they watched for offenses as small as wearing red and white (colors associated with secession).

Someone put a Union flag on the front of the O'Flaherty house. Kate took it down, hiding it in a scrap bag. Soldiers arrived and demanded to know where the flag was. Suspecting Kate knew more than she was saying, they threatened to arrest her. Only the intervention of a neighbor, a known Union supporter, saved her. The story spread around the city, and Kate was quickly hailed by those who sided with the South as the "littlest rebel."

During the war, Kate suffered several losses. Madame Charleville died in January of 1863; her half-brother George died the next month; and her best friend Kitty moved away after her father was forced to leave St. Louis because he refused to take an oath of loyalty to the Union. Kitty and Kate didn't meet again for several years.

Kate continued her schooling with the nuns, winning prizes and honors for her abilities. One nun in particular, Madam Mary O'Meara, saw special talent in her student and encouraged Kate to write. Kate began keeping a commonplace book, a sort of scrapbook in which she jotted down quotations or literary passages she'd found, often adding her own comments and compositions—a practice she would continue sporadically throughout her life.

Upon graduation, Kate formally entered St. Louis society. An attractive young woman with a mass of dark curls and dark brown eyes, she was noted for her intelligence. Kitty, too, now back in St. Louis, was happily preparing for her debut as well. Her joy, however, was cut short with the sudden death of her father. She withdrew from society, in keeping with mourning customs of the time—and she never returned. Instead, Kitty joined the Sisters of the Sacred Heart, and Kate again lost her best friend.

With mixed pleasure, Kate participated in a busy whirl of parties and festivities, She found the activities tiring, and they left little time for reading and reflection. She wrote in her diary that it took little effort for a young woman to be admired by young men. "All required of you is to have control over the muscles of your face—to look pleased and cha-grined, surprised indignant and under every circumstance—interested and entertained." While Kate entranced the young men who enjoyed talking about themselves, she took pride in keeping her own thoughts and feelings private.

For almost a year Kate wrote nothing in her diary. Then, on May 24, 1870, she began again. It must have been a busy year because the entry contained the statement, "in two weeks I am going to be married." The groom-to-be was Oscar Chopin, great-nephew of Louis A. Benoist, a wealthy St. Louis banker.

Oscar's family had considerable land in northwestern Louisiana. His father was a doctor—and a tyrant, abusing both his wife and his slaves. When the Civil War started, Doctor Chopin took his family to France, leaving his estates in the care of neighbors.

Following the war, Oscar returned to the United States, going to St. Louis to learn business from his great uncle. Louis Benoist owned a mansion in St. Louis and a country home, named Oakland, where many social events took place. Evidently, Kate and Oscar met on one of these occasions.

Kate and Oscar made a good pair. Perhaps from his years in Europe or perhaps because of his disgust with his father's treatment of his mother, Oscar didn't seem to mind Kate's independent streak. Though the couple enjoyed many things in common, Kate needed time to herself. Even on their extended honeymoon, Kate went walking alone, went rowing, enjoyed a beer by herself, and smoked cigarettes—none of which would have been acceptable in St. Louis at the time. After a three-month honeymoon, Oscar and Kate stopped briefly in St. Louis before journeying to New Orleans, where they would make their home and prepare for the birth of their first child.

Kate enjoyed New Orleans but missed her mother. Mother and daughter visited back and forth, staying weeks, even months at a time. Kate had help at home, and when she wasn't pregnant, she was able to get out. She took long walks and recorded her impressions in a little notebook. She reveled in the warmth, colors, and sounds of the city—a sophisticated place with many cultural opportunities.

In those days, when it became obvious a woman was expecting a baby, it was no longer considered proper for her to be seen in public. It must have been frustrating for freedom-loving Kate, particularly since she was pregnant many times—giving birth to five children during a span of less than seven years. Kate and Oscar's first son, Jean, was born in May 1871. Oscar Charles was born a year later, followed by George in late 1874. Frederick arrived in January of 1876, and Felix was born two years to the month later.

Despite her numerous "confinements," Kate and Oscar had many friends and entertained frequently. Oscar was a good husband and father. He was easygoing, was not a stern disciplinarian, and enjoyed playing with the children. Kate—who was not bound by convention or what others thought—continued to enjoy solitary strolls, exploring the city, and smoking in public.

The family spent summers at the seaside on Grand Isle, a tiny barrier island off the coast of Louisiana. Wives and children would flock to the isle to escape the heat of New Orleans and the danger of diseases.

Husbands and fathers would come down to join them on the weekends. The climate was more comfortable, the vegetation was lush and exotic, and the children could run and play in the water. Kate would use this bucolic setting in her most important work, *The Awakening*.

All in all, Kate led a pleasant, if harried, life in New Orleans, but things did not go well with her husband's business. Oscar had become a cotton factor, a middleman between cotton producers and cotton buyers, and the crops had done poorly for several years. Unlike most husbands, Oscar discussed his business with his wife. They decided to leave New Orleans and settle in Natchitoches Parish, where Oscar had inherited land from his father. Their sixth child and only daughter, Lélia, was born in Natchitoches in 1879.

If Kate had been slightly out of place in bustling St. Louis and sophisticated New Orleans, she was about to set the tiny village of Cloutierville (pronounced CLUE-chee-ville) on its ear. The hamlet consisted of a dusty main street and rows of small, plain wood houses. The Chopin family moved into one of the largest homes, a two-story brick and cypress structure that had belonged to the founder of the town. Oscar was related to a number of people in the area; Kate, too, had relatives in the vicinity. Related or not, everyone knew everybody else's business and didn't hesitate to discuss it.

Kate's solitary walks, riding bareback and astride a horse, smoking cigarettes, wearing daring outfits, and her "Yankee ways" brought criticism and condemnation. Oscar and Kate only laughed at the comments, with Kate often mimicking her critics to Oscar in private.

Oscar purchased a store in Cloutierville and became a storekeeper. He was very popular, being that he was generous in extending credit and reluctant to pursue payment. Kate often helped in the business, which allowed her to become acquainted with the town's characters and secrets—providing fodder for her future work, though she didn't realize that at the time.

The meandering Cane River flowed near Cloutierville. The area's bayous and swamps harbored mosquitoes, a source of malaria, and many residents—including Oscar—suffered from recurring attacks. The disease, which the local doctor diagnosed as "swamp fever," seemed to come and go. His worst attack came in late 1882, and on December 10, Oscar died, leaving his grieving wife with six children and more than twelve thousand dollars in debts.

Unlike most widows of the day, Kate did not turn to any of the gentlemen who offered to help her sort out her affairs. Instead, she rolled up her sleeves, worked in the store, hounded customers for payments, sold some land and property, and oversaw the remaining plantations. Within a year and a half, she had settled her financial obligations.

If men, both single and married, had been interested in helping Kate right after Oscar's death, they were even more interested when she came out of mourning. She enjoyed having a good time and angered many of the local ladies by flirting openly.

One of her admirers was a local planter—married, with a reputation as a rake. Albert Sampite and his wife were not well-matched. He was social and enjoyed gambling, drinking, and partying; she enjoyed staying home. Albert and Kate had many opportunities to be together and were the subject of gossip. Many in town were relieved when, in 1884, Kate and her children moved back to St. Louis.

Among Kate's reasons for the move was her desire for a good education for her children. She also had more family in St. Louis than Louisiana, and she had never really fit into the community in Cloutierville.

Kate was home about a year when her mother died. With her inheritance and the rent from her Louisiana properties, she had the means to move into a larger house in a newer part of town. In addition to family and old friends, Kate was meeting new ones. She had known Doctor Frederick Kolbenheyer before—he had delivered two of her children; now, he became an important influence. Not surprisingly, considering all she had been through, Kate suffered from depression, Doctor Kolbenheyer gave her a prescription for it: He encouraged Kate to write.

At about this time, Kate also discovered a writer who inspired her—Guy de Maupassant. She considered his topics and his treatment of them to be "real"; others considered him obscene. Maupassant was French, and America was not. His writing dealt with situations "nice" people didn't discuss—a criticism that would later be thrown at Kate.

In 1888, Kate published her first written piece—a piano composition. Her first literary publication, a poem, appeared in January 1889, and her first short story appeared in the *St. Louis Post Dispatch* in October of that year.

She was remarkably disciplined and organized in her work. She usually had several projects going at once and kept careful records of submissions, rejections or acceptances, and payments.

Her first book was titled *At Fault* and dealt with divorce. When it failed to find a publisher, Kate published it herself in 1890. The book received local reviews as well as one in New Orleans and one national review. Like many of Kate's works, it was open to many interpretations. It also exhibited a practice that became a hallmark of her writing: She borrowed a great deal from real life—including people, names, places, and events. Sometimes characters were well disguised; at other times, her characters were easily recognized by others.

Although Kate, by virtue of her birth and upbringing, was part of St. Louis society, she was more interested in the world of ideas. She was invited to become a charter member of the Wednesday Club, a group of influential St. Louis women, but resigned after two years. She, instead, surrounded herself with a coterie of people whom her son Felix described as a "liberal, almost pink-red group of intellectuals." They met regularly at her home—the equivalent of a European salon.

During this productive period of almost ten years, Kate produced a prodigious number of stories. Sometimes she wrote what editors wanted—stories suitable for young people—but increasingly, she pushed the boundaries with stories of relationships and of love within and outside of marriage. She wrote about childbirth, and she wrote one story from the point of view of a black woman—things unheard of in women's writing of the time. She also made enemies with the people on which her characters were based.

A recurring theme in her work was the conflict between women's roles as defined by society and women's abilities and ambitions. She was already making a national reputation as a writer when she began work on a novel that explored this dilemma in depth—*The Awakening*. The main character, Edna Pontillier, was twenty-eight years old, married, and the mother of two children. Her husband, twelve years her senior, provided well for his family. In the context of society at that time, Edna should have been happy, but *The Awakening* explores Edna's dissatisfaction with and search for greater meaning in her life.

When the book was released in April 1899, it caused an uproar. Reviewers used words like "vulgar," "trite and sordid," and "it leaves one sick of human nature." Although it received some positive reviews and Kate's friends rallied around her, the criticism stung.

Contrary to popular belief, *The Awakening* was never banned by the St. Louis libraries and Kate was not kicked out of women's clubs. In fact, she was honored by the Wednesday Club, being included in a program entitled "An Afternoon with St. Louis Authors." She was listed in the 1900 edition (the first year of its publication) of *Who's Who in America*.

Following the release of *The Awakening*, Kate wrote less frequently and published few pieces. Perhaps the decline in her work was due to her involvement in Lelia's social debut, or her disappointment with the reception of *The Awakening*, or her failing health. Her last published piece, a short story called "Polly's Opportunity," appeared in *Youth's Companion* in July, 1902.

In 1904, St. Louis hosted the World's Fair. Officially known as the Louisiana Purchase Exposition, it was a showcase of innovation and a wonderland of exhibits from all over the world. Kate attended on opening day, April 30, and visited almost daily. After spending the day at the fair on August 20—a typical sweltering St. Louis summer day—Kate was hot and tired. Late that night she complained of a sharp pain in her head and lost consciousness. She died two days later, August 22, from an apparent cerebral hemorrhage.

Kate and her notorious book faded into obscurity for decades. Then, in the 1960s, Harvard doctoral candidate Per Seyersted made Kate and her works the subject of his dissertation. His research and subsequent publication of her complete works led to her rediscovery. Today, Kate Chopin is recognized for her literary style as well as for her insight and honesty in exploring women's feelings.

ALICE BERRY GRAHAM
(1850–1913)

KATHARINE BERRY RICHARDSON
(1858–1933)

MOTHERS OF MERCY

On the night of June 1, 1897, Doctor Alice Berry Graham answered the phone to hear a voice say, "Come quick, there's a mother down here trying to give away her little girl." It was a saloonkeeper in the West Bottoms area of Kansas City—not a good place for a woman alone at night. The area housed the stockyards and the train depot along with the hotels and saloons where cattlemen and drummers collected and caroused on summer evenings. Despite the danger, Alice ventured out and found the five-year-old child, a cripple, and her mother in a room behind a dance hall. Confronted by the indignant doctor about her lack of care for the girl, the mother complained she was tired of the child's "bawling." Borrowing a shawl to wrap up the dirty, ragged little girl, she took the child from her mother and brought her back to the office building where Alice and her sister, Doctor Katharine Berry Richardson, worked and lived.

Once the two doctors had cleaned up the little girl, they addressed the problem of what to do with her. They ended up taking her to a small maternity hospital where they were able to rent a bed. Doctor Richardson operated on the child's injured hip, and once she'd recovered, placed her in an orphanage.

After helping a second abandoned child, the two sisters realized they had found a shared mission that became a lifelong effort to aid poor,

Alice Berry Graham Courtesy of Children's Mercy Hospital and Clinics, Kansas City, MO

sick children. A dream that began with one child in a rented hospital bed dream grew into one of the nation's top children's hospitals—Children's Mercy Hospital in Kansas City, Missouri.

That's a great story and it may be true. In another account, one that seems to be verified by a 1924 newspaper article, Katharine described their first charity patient differently: She told of Alice finding a crying baby in a trash bin. Lack of verifiable documentation makes it difficult to tell the history of these two remarkable women with accuracy. Chances are, both of these incidents happened at one time or another. The plight of poor children at the turn of the last century was desperate, and the sisters could have related many heartbreaking accounts.

Details of the sisters' early years are sketchy, too. Their parents were Harriet Benson and Stephen Berry. Alice was born on March 3, 1850, in North Warren, Pennsylvania. Shortly afterward, the family moved to Flat Rock, Kentucky, where Stephen owned property and ran a grist mill. A second daughter, Claire or Clara, was born in Kentucky, as was the last child, Katharine, who was born on September 28, 1858.

Stephen was known to be a man of strong opinions and great respect for the responsibilities of citizenship. The girls never forgot his tutelage, and years later Katharine could still recall his words: "The responsibility of an American extends beyond his own family. Wherever you go it is your duty to make good citizens of your neighbors."

During the Civil War, the Berrys were Union sympathizers but lived in a community loyal to the South. Everyone in the community was expected to take an oath pledging allegiance to the Southern cause. Stephen not only refused, he also tacked a notice on the mill door stating that he was a Union supporter. Angry neighbors put a bounty on his life, and he was forced to flee to Ohio, where he joined the Union army, leaving his wife and children in Kentucky.

Harriet, too, held strong convictions and sympathized with the Union. Confederate supporters had taken possession of the mill and were operating it. In the dark of night, Harriet removed parts of the machinery, which she then buried. The mill would grind no grain to support the insurrection!

Following the war, Stephen returned to Kentucky. Harriet had died in his absence, leaving nothing for him there. He took the three girls and returned to Pennsylvania. He had little money then and never managed to make much more, but he insisted that his daughters receive an education.

In keeping with the popular sentiment of the time—that girls were expected to become good wives and mothers only—the middle daughter, Claire, married. Alice and Katharine, however, finished school and prepared for college. Since they had no money for college, the two agreed that Alice would take the teachers' examination and teach school to pay for Katharine's tuition. Katharine earned both bachelor's and master's degrees from Mount Union College in Ohio; she then went on to the Woman's Medical College of Pennsylvania. In addition to her studies, Kate tutored other students to help pay her way. She graduated with her medical degree in 1887.

Now it was Alice's turn. Katharine taught school while Alice completed a dental degree at the Philadelphia Dental College.

Huge pieces to the puzzle of Alice and Katharine's lives before their coming to Kansas City in the mid-1890s are missing. Alice married and became widowed during the time between Katharine leaving for school and both women leaving for Kansas City. Upon Katharine's graduation, the two sisters decided to settle in the west. Katharine would go first and Alice would join her after she finished school. To settle the question of location, they dropped a coin on a map of the United States. It landed on La Crosse, Wisconsin.

In 1893, Katharine married Doctor James Richardson, a dentist who practiced in Eau Claire, about ninety miles north of La Crosse. Why and exactly when the Richardsons and Alice moved to Kansas City is unknown.

Katharine Berry Richardson Courtesy of Children's Mercy Hospital and Clinics, Kansas City, MO

Upon their arrival, they rented space in an office building in downtown Kansas City, where they not only hung their shingles but also made their home. Many obstacles stood in the way of their success, not the least of which being the attitude of the medical and dental communities. Women were considered an oddity and definitely not welcomed. With careful planning and frugal habits, Alice and Katharine managed to eke out a living in their chosen professions. For example, they rose early and aired out the rooms so their patients wouldn't smell the breakfast bacon when they arrived.

Through events in 1897, the sisters saw the tremendous need of the poor in the community. Impoverished people couldn't afford health care, and even if they could, few hospital beds for sick children were available. Pediatrics was a relatively new field. Until the Civil War, infant care had been considered part of obstetrics. Children were treated as little adults and simply received scaled-down services.

As Alice and Katharine found more needy children, they realized their meager resources would soon be exhausted. They needed their own hospital. They had been renting beds in a small maternity hospital run by a group of women. The hospital was about to go under financially, but the lease was not up for another year. The doctors knew the licensing board would never grant a license for a general hospital run by women, so they made arrangements to take over the lease and very quietly began to change the focus of the institution. Soon the women had a dozen beds filled with indigent expectant mothers and children.

No other hospital in town would take these poor patients. Although some male physicians did send patients there, the women still remained unrecognized or helped by the medical community. The community in general ignored them—except for a mocking cartoon in a local newspaper. Doctor Richardson, wearing an apron and a towel wrapped around her head, was depicted standing on a stool simultaneously cleaning and directing the activities of others below. The caption read: "Only women. A hospital from which men are to be entirely excluded."

The two doctors did perform housekeeping chores along with the other women staff members—anything to save money. They both devoted themselves to the hospital, taking only a couple of hours a day to see their private, paying patients.

With the lease for the rickety building at Fifteenth and Cleveland about to expire, the doctors needed to find another place for their patients. They were able to rent space in another women's hospital at Eleventh and Troost, but then that lease ended as well. So they farmed out patients to private homes and made house calls until other arrangements could be made.

They were at their funds' end—but not their wits' end. They began speaking to groups throughout the area and soliciting donations from anyone who would listen to them. They finally accumulated enough money to buy a large home, which had once been the residence of former Kansas City mayor R. H Hunt. Their hospital, first known as the Hospital of the Free Bed Association, opened with five beds on January 1, 1904. Over the next two years, the capacity expanded to accommodate twenty-seven patients and the sign in front of the building was changed to read MERCY HOSPITAL. Doctor Richardson paid tribute to her sister in the inscription on the cornerstone: "In 1897, Dr. Alice Berry Graham founded this hospital for sick and crippled children to be forever non-sectarian, non-local, and for those who cannot pay."

Doctor Graham took over many of the business functions of the hospital, while Doctor Richardson served as primary physician and surgeon. Doctor Graham, in a brilliant combination of education and solicitation, produced a monthly mailer, the *Mercy Messenger*. Larger than a postcard and of heavy paper stock so it would hold up to being passed around, the piece usually featured an ill or crippled child—sometimes before and after photographs—and information on the hospital. It also included child-care tips for mothers.

Fund-raising was an ongoing task. Eventually, Mercy Clubs—groups of supporters from across the region—were started, adding to the hospital's financial resources. Doctor Richardson adamantly insisted that the hospital would accept no money that was not a free gift and would not spend money it did not have. When the time came to build a new hospital, the construction was stopped several times and did not restart until funds had been procured.

The year 1908 was a difficult one for the sisters. Doctor James Richardson, Katharine's husband, who had been an invalid for several years, died, and Doctor Graham was diagnosed with cancer. Through her battle with the disease, she continued soliciting funds for the hospital—making public appearances as long as she could, contacting the Mercy Clubs, and writing *Mercy Messenger*.

Doctor Richardson kept her hands firmly on the reins of the hospital as it grew in reputation and size. She stuck to her guns, even when doing so might have seemed counterproductive. At one point, she received a visit from a prominent businessman and his lawyer. The gentleman had what he considered to be an extremely generous offer: He volunteered to take complete financial responsibility for the hospital. There was just one condition—that the name Mercy be dropped and the institution named after him and his wife. Doctor Richardson's "No, thank you," came firmly and bluntly. "I would never change the name of Mercy," she told him. "Many people have contributed to this hospital. I wouldn't name it for myself or even for my sister. The name must remain Mercy—the people's hospital." The businessman and his lawyer left shaking their heads.

Doctor Richardson, dedicated to her children and her hospital, refused to be cowed even by the most intimidating interrogator—not even the politically powerful and wealthy newspaper publisher William

Rockhill Nelson. He was the type of man who, when he said "Jump," expected a response of "How high?" One one occasion, he requested that Doctor Kate come to the newspaper office. When she entered the room, he did not rise and instead greeted her with a curt, "Sit down, young lady."

Kate complied, and Nelson began questioning her, pointing out that his newspaper had given her a great deal of free publicity. "I want to find out about you," he told her. He asked what she had been doing with all the money she had been collecting, seemingly calling the legitimacy of her operation into question. Kate still had enough red in her graying hair to quickly stand and tell him off. She gave him a brief summary of her background, education, and early experience in Kansas City. She spoke heatedly about the condition of poor and crippled children in the city and what the hospital was doing for them. She ended by challenging him to send someone to verify what she had said. With that, she stormed out of the office, thinking she had made an enemy.

Nelson did check out everything she had told him. He not only published her story, he also continued to publish stories about the needs of the hospital and its little patients.

One of those needs was a bigger hospital. The hospital on Highland had become so crowded that the staff was putting two, sometimes three, children in each bed. In memory of his daughter, a local businessman, Jemuel Clinton Gates, donated a two-acre plot on the corner of Woodland and Independence Boulevard. By this time, Alice was quite ill, but she and Katharine, along with their supporters, began raising money for a new structure. It was a lengthy process, and Alice did not live long enough to see the start of construction. Doctor Alice Berry Graham died on May 3, 1913. The new Mercy Hospital opened in 1917.

Over the years, Doctor Richardson and Doctor Graham had broken many barriers—among them, opening a training school for nurses. A century ago, nurses were not held in high esteem, and nursing was not considered a proper career for "nice" women. In England, Florence Nightingale had worked hard to change this opinion, becoming famous during the mid-1800s as the "Lady with the Lamp" during the Crimean War. Afterward, she wrote extensively on hospital administration, nurses' training, and reforming the health care system.

Doctor Graham and Doctor Richardson insisted on high standards from their nurses. It took two years for a girl to complete the course. The nurses were expected to be clean and tidy at all times with properly laundered and ironed uniforms. Their long dresses were blue gingham with long, white aprons. Their caps were designed, at Katharine's request, by Florence Nightingale herself.

One of the ongoing concerns of both women was the lack of facilities for black children. This was a time of strict segregation and prejudice, and many staff members balked at treating the black children. Although Doctor Richardson designated one bed in the new hospital on Independence for a critically ill child regardless of race, she knew that was woefully inadequate. Working with a local black doctor who had a small facility, she arranged for several black physicians to come to Mercy to train in pediatrics. She also talked some of her nurses into training black nurses to work specifically with children. While asking for donations for her own hospital, she also asked people for money for what would become the Wheatley-Provident Hospital, the only black-owned facility of its kind in the Midwest.

Until the end of her days, Doctor Richardson refused to take a salary for her work at Mercy. "If I can be hired, I can be fired," she said, "and I plan to work until I die." She also refused to tell her age, saying, "If you tell your age . . . they will want to retire you." She never retired. While preparing her schedule on June 2, 1933, she suddenly doubled over in pain, and she died the following evening.

Two years before her death, she was awarded an honorary Doctor of Law degree from Mount Union College. The president of the school paid her this tribute: "Had Union College done nothing but turned out a Katharine B. Richardson, all the sacrifice and hardships of the past would be repaid." Today, Children's Mercy Hospital, now located at Twenty-fourth Street and Gillham Road, stands as a monument to these two amazing sisters, doctors, and women—Alice Berry Graham and Katharine Berry Richardson.

LAURA INGALLS WILDER

(1867–1957)

AMERICA'S MOST POPULAR PIONEER

Although she experienced almost as many disasters as Pharaoh, Laura Ingalls Wilder considered her life a happy one. And it was a long life—spanning ninety years and a time in American history that progressed from covered wagons to jet planes, campfires to central heating, and tell a neighbor to telephones.

Laura is most famous for telling her own story of growing up on America's Western frontier. The Missouri author did this in a series known as the "Little House" books, which have been favorites with children around the world for more than seventy-five years.

Like a braid, Laura's life story has three strands: the actual facts, the facts tweaked for her books, and the television version. It's easy to get confused. The changes to events that she made for the books are insignificant; they simply make the stories easier to follow.

Laura was born in Wisconsin in 1867. Her parents were Caroline Quiner and Charles Ingalls, whom she always called Ma and Pa. Both the Quiner and Ingalls families had been part of the great American pioneering movement, leaving New England and moving farther and farther west. This pattern of "moving on" was a hallmark of Laura's youth.

Although she didn't have the stability of location, she certainly had stability of character—the result of a happy, close family and sound grounding in the importance of honesty, integrity, frugality, perseverance, and generosity. Add to these qualities a keen sense of humor and the ability to see the silver lining on the darkest of clouds, and Laura was equipped to successfully deal with the vicissitudes of life.

Laura Ingalls Wilder Courtesy of Laura Ingalls Wilder Home Association, Mansfield, MO

After the end of the Civil War in 1865, the country experienced a surge of westward movement. Charles Ingalls had itchy feet, and the family headed south and west from Wisconsin—the first of many moves. By 1868 or 1869, Charles, Caroline, Laura, and her sister Mary, who was two years older than Laura, were living in southeast Kansas. This was Osage land, and the Indians resented settlement on their territory, making the family's stay in Kansas short. While they were there, Laura's and Mary's sister Carrie was born.

Carrie was just a babe in arms when the family packed up their wagon and began the long, arduous trip back to Wisconsin. On a good day they could travel only twenty miles, and the trip was over six hundred miles long. Laura was about six years old when they reached the house in which she had been born—a little house in the big woods near Pepin, Wisconsin.

It took the whole family working together to make things run smoothly. Laura's days were filled with activity whether it was milking the cow, or making butter, or just staying out of the way during butchering season. Years later, as Laura remembered how rich and interesting her childhood had been, she wanted to tell younger generations what it was like growing up on the frontier.

It wasn't all work. After the hog butchering, an inflated bladder served as a ball, and a corncob wrapped in a piece of cloth made a wonderful doll. In the evening, when the day's work was done, Ma and Pa would read or tell stories to the children. Many evenings, Pa would take down his fiddle and play and sing, and Laura often went to sleep with the sweet sound of the strings floating through the little house.

Grandparents, aunts, uncles, and cousins also lived in the area, and whenever family members were able to get together, it was a celebration. Neighbors were few and far between, but everyone pitched in when someone needed help.

Although the family was happy to be with old friends and relatives, their stay in Wisconsin lasted only a few years before Charles Ingalls was ready to move on again. The land was getting crowded, and he longed for the open prairies. Railroads were moving farther and farther west, and where the railroad went, little settlements grew up around new depots. Walnut Grove, Minnesota, was one of those settlements, and that's where the Ingalls family ended up.

Charles worked hard building a house and planting crops. Two disastrous years followed. As the crops were ripening, clouds of grass-hoppers descended on them, stripping the fields more efficiently than any modern mower. Like a blanket, they covered everything. Even the wheels on the trains slipped when rolling over the mass of insects. Mean-while, Caroline had a new baby, Freddie, and the family needed money.

Laura skipped over the next period of her life when she wrote her books. Her little brother Freddie died, and the family moved to Burr Oak, Iowa, where Charles became part owner of a hotel. During this time, Laura's third sister, Grace, was born.

In the hotel, both Mary and Laura helped in the kitchen and din-ing room, swept, and made beds. Charles, in addition to helping run the hotel, ran a mill and worked at other odd jobs. With more mouths to feed, even with everyone working hard, there just didn't seem to be enough money to make ends meet. So the family moved again, returning to Walnut Grove, Minnesota.

Without a farm, Charles found work clerking in a store, then later running a small butcher shop and working as a carpenter. Laura helped supplement the family's income by working in a local hotel, sweeping, making beds, washing dishes, and babysitting. During this period in Walnut Grove, Mary went blind, probably as the result of a stroke related to an earlier bout with measles. Laura, now twelve, became Mary's eyes. Laura had always been good with language, and Mary often referred to Laura's descriptions as pictures painted with words.

Life was again proving difficult when fate, in the form of Charles' sister Ladocia, provided the impetus for the next move. Her husband, who worked for the railroad, needed someone to keep the crew records and to run the railroad store while the crew extended the rail line into South Dakota. The pay was good, and Charles knew that homesteaders in the area could receive land in exchange for living on it and working it for several years. They took the train, a new experience for Laura, to the end of the line and then traveled by wagon to their new home in what would become DeSmet, South Dakota.

This would be Laura's home for more than a decade and her mother's and father's home for the rest of their lives. It also was where Laura first met Almanzo Wilder, a young man who was homesteading with his brother near DeSmet. He and another young man saved the citizens of DeSmet in the winter of 1880, when the snow was so deep and the blizzards so fierce that no trains with supplies could reach the town. The two men traveled miles through the snow to find a farmer who had some extra grain.

Meanwhile, Laura was growing up and earning a reputation as a scholar. Even though she was only fifteen, a year under the legal age for teachers, she was offered an eight-week teaching contract at a little school twelve miles away. Laura didn't want to leave her own school and her family, but the offer of twenty dollars a month was too good to pass up. Laura's parents had heard of a school for the blind in Iowa, and Laura's salary would help pay Mary's tuition.

Although both her mother and grandmother had been teachers, Laura wasn't anxious to follow in their footsteps. Her inexperience, youth, and stature—she was only five feet tall—presented obstacles, but once she had signed her contract, there was no turning back. She soon learned to manage her classroom.

The school was a simple, one-room building with a coal-burning stove for warmth. The winter winds blew fiercely across the prairie, and snow blew through the cracks in the walls—and that was probably the warmest part of her day.

When she accepted the teaching position, it was arranged that she would room with a local family, the Bouchies. Laura soon discovered that Mrs. Bouchie was a sour, dissatisfied woman who resented living in the area. Because she was miserable, Mrs. Bouchie did everything she could to make sure everyone else suffered, too. Laura often retreated to her bed early to escape the chilly atmosphere among the family members.

Laura was depressed because she knew her father could not get all his work done and manage the four twelve-mile trips it would take to bring her home on the weekends. So you can imagine her surprise when, at the end of the school day on Friday of her first week on the job, she heard the jingle of bells. It was Almanzo Wilder with his sleigh and team of swift horses. He'd come to take her home, and this became a regular event that considerably brightened her two-month assignment.

Almanzo was ten years older than Laura, and while she'd had good friends who were boys, she'd never thought of Almanzo as a possible beau. Although she didn't want him to stop picking her up, neither did she want to give him "ideas" and explained to him that she appreciated the rides—but that was all. So she was a little surprised when, like clockwork, Almanzo was outside the school the next Friday afternoon.

When Laura's assignment was over, she returned home and back to her own schooling. Spring was coming, and with the snow melting, there were no more sleigh rides. Then one day Almanzo showed up with a shiny new buggy. Laura had missed the tall, quiet man and soon found herself looking forward to Sunday afternoons, when they would ride about the countryside. It was only a matter of time before Almanzo proposed and Laura accepted. On their wedding day, August 25, 1885, the bride was eighteen and the groom twenty-eight. At Laura's insistence, the word "obey" was omitted from the ceremony.

Here would be a perfect stopping spot in the tale—a "they lived happily ever after" moment. Half a century later when Laura finished *These Happy Golden Years,* she ended her stories at this point.

But life went on, and it was full of difficulties. Being the mistress of her own house was very different from being a daughter in a large family, and Almanzo did things differently from Charles Ingalls. Charles never bought anything he couldn't pay for immediately. Ambitious and hard-working, Almanzo invested in machinery to make the farm work easier. When his crops yielded less income than he'd expected, he found his credit was overextended and the family was in a financial bind.

Their first child, Rose, was born in December of 1886. Although the next year's wheat harvest was good, their barn burned down with their grain and hay in it. Laura and Almanzo worked hard to keep their heads above water, but things just seemed to go from bad to worse. Early in 1888, both Almanzo and Laura contracted diphtheria, and in its after-math, Almanzo suffered a stroke from which he never completely recovered. The next year, 1889, brought another series of tragedies: Drought devastated their crops. Laura had a second baby, a little boy, who died when he was only twelve days old. Two weeks later, their house burned down. The couple moved to Minnesota to live with Almanzo's parents while they decided what to do next.

The next few years mirrored Laura's first few years, with the family making several long-distance moves. They tried Florida, hoping the warmer weather would benefit Almanzo's health. It didn't; the heat and humidity were so unpleasant that they moved back to South Dakota temporarily before moving on once more.

Not even two years later, in 1894, having heard good reports about land in Missouri, Almanzo and Laura packed a wagon and with their daughter Rose began the long trek to Missouri. The trip took nearly six weeks. Arriving in the Ozarks, in the far southwestern corner of the state, Laura was taken with the hills and trees. Fifty miles east of Spring-field, they discovered the little town of Mansfield. After days of search-ing, Almanzo found forty acres for sale east of town. The Wilders had come home.

They named the place Rocky Ridge—an apt description of the topography. The soil was good, but the best crop seemed to be rocks. The former owners had managed to clear only four acres. Working with a cross cut saw, Almanzo and Laura cleared more acres. Although Almanzo's stroke made it impossible for him to work the land as he had once done, he and Laura made good partners. The first two years, the family managed by selling firewood they had cut and eggs from the chickens Laura raised.

While Laura could help with all sorts of chores, even driving a team of six horses to pull farm machinery, she believed adamantly that a woman's role was that of homemaker and mother. Her own role as a mother was frequently frustrating; she and Rose were often at odds. Intellectually brilliant but difficult and temperamental, Rose was her mother's delight and despair.

As the years went by, the farm grew more prosperous and the family more financially comfortable. Laura was never extravagant with money, and Rose chaffed under what she considered her mother's penny-pinching ways. She also balked at Laura's rules and strictures, later complaining, "Her character is Scotch; she holds a purpose or opinion like granite."

By the time she was sixteen, Rose was thoroughly bored with school and ready to quit. It was probably with a sigh of relief mixed with sadness that Laura agreed to let Rose live with Almanzo's sister Eliza to finish school in Crowley, Louisiana. Rose sped through her studies, finishing four years of Latin in one year. After graduating at age seventeen, she moved to Kansas City to work as a telegraph operator. She was independent, determined, and adventuresome—characteristics she shared with her mother and that led her to opportunities that would take her all over the world.

Laura, with these same traits, had settled happily into life at Rocky Ridge. Up to this point, her life, as full of excitement and challenges as it had been, had not been dissimilar to the lives of hundreds of other women of her day. Resilience and optimism were survival skills for pioneers.

Although the family's moving days were over, Laura's lively mind and innate leadership ability kept her busy with community activities— church associations, study clubs, social gatherings—but she seemed happiest on the farm. One of her favorite tasks was raising chickens, and she became such an expert that she was invited to speak on the subject at an agricultural meeting. Unable to attend, she wrote out her speech and sent it for someone else to read. The editor of a farm journal, *The Missouri Ruralist,* attended the meeting. He contacted her to suggest she submit something to the paper, and her first published article appeared on February 18, 1911.

Rose, keenly aware of her position as an only child and concerned about her parents' financial future, encouraged her mother's writing. Laura wrote sporadically at first but was eventually given her own bimonthly column. Her subjects, aimed at farm women, ranged from household tips and beauty advice to the environment and the world situation.

Rose, also a talented writer whose work was published regularly, suggested Laura try writing pieces for major magazines. Laura would send penciled drafts to Rose, who would edit, type, and submit them to editors. Occasionally, Laura would send a children's story, but Rose wasn't interested in those, saying there was no future in writing for children.

In 1930, probably as a result of Rose's prodding, Laura wrote an autobiography. Rose thought it might sell to a magazine for serialization—a common practice of the time in which magazines bought books and printed them in several issues. "To be continued" at the end of a chapter ensured the reader would buy the next issue.

At the same time, Laura and Rose turned some of the material into a short story. Among the people to whom Rose sent copies was a friend,

Berta Hader, a noted children's book illustrator. Who knows what Rose had in mind, given that she had been so dismissive of children's literature, but in any event, Berta loved the story and passed it on to Marion Fiery, an editor at a book publishing company. Fiery was impressed with the piece, and he was prepared to offer Laura a contract when the publishing company decided to close its juvenile division. Fiery was probably responsible for the book winding up on the desk of Virginia Kirkus at Harper and Brothers. The rest is, literally, history.

Laura was now sixty-five years old, and her life was about to change dramatically. *Little House in the Big Woods* came out in 1932, and it was a big hit with both critics and children. Her book about Almanzo's youth, *Farmer Boy,* was published in 1933, and followed in 1935 by *Little House on the Prairie. On the Banks of Plum Creek* appeared on shelves in 1937, *By the Shores of Silver Lake* in 1939, *The Long Winter* in 1940, *Little Town on the Prairie* in 1941, and *These Happy Golden Years* in 1943. By then, Laura was famous and in great demand for personal appearances, most of which she declined.

(The last book in the Little House series, *The First Four Years,* was probably written and abandoned early in the 1930s. Years after Laura's death, when Rose died, three tablets with the draft of the book were found among her things. Rose's friend and advisor Roger Lea McBride inherited them and published them in 1972.)

Laura had completed the eight-book series she had planned, and its popularity continued to grow. In the meantime, she and Almanzo were growing old. In July of 1948, when Laura was eighty-one and Almanzo ninety-one, he suffered a serious heart attack that left him incapacitated. A second heart attack in October of that year was fatal. After sixty-four years of marriage, Laura was alone.

Laura remained at Rocky Ridge. Her books were as popular as ever, and she received thousands of letters from her fans. She never owned a television set and spent most of her time reading, embroidering, crocheting, or playing solitaire. She had some friends and enjoyed an occasional lunch out. She even accepted Rose's invitation to visit her in Connecticut, taking her first plane ride at the age of eighty-seven.

Having witnessed the transformation of a nation from its pioneer past to a position of world power, Laura Ingalls Wilder died a few days before her ninetieth birthday and is buried beside Almanzo in the Mansfield Cemetery. To millions of readers, she will always be young—a spunky, brown-haired, blue-eyed youngster whose stories gave a better picture of frontier life than any history book ever written.

ROSE CECIL O'NEILL

(1874–1944)

ILLUSTRIOUS ILLUSTRATOR

"**N**o thirteen-year-old girl could draw this!" That was the reaction of the editors at the *Omaha World-Herald* who were judging entries in the newspaper's contest for the best drawing by a Nebraska youngster. The entry in question—an elaborate pen-and-ink illustration entitled "Temptation Leading Down into an Abyss"—was certainly not what one would expect of a child's artwork. But then, the editors had never met Rose O'Neill.

Almost nothing about Rose's life was conventional. As unusual as her upbringing was, one big fact made everything work: Rose and her brothers and sisters were surrounded with love and respect.

Rose's father, William Patrick O'Neill, Irish to the bone and larger than life, had big ideas and little practicality. Rose described her Papa as "a romantic with lucid moments." Her mother, Alice Aseneth Cecelia Smith O'Neill, known as Meemie, had been a teacher before her marriage and sang and played the piano beautifully.

Rose was born on June 25, 1874, in Wilkes-Barre, Pennsylvania, where William owned a bookstore and art gallery and Rose enjoyed a fairy-tale childhood. The family—Papa, Meemie, Rose's older brother Hugh, and Rose—lived in a cozy cottage trimmed with Victorian gingerbread. Called Emerald Cottage, the charming little house sported painted cherubs cavorting on the ceiling of the octagonal drawing room and was surrounded by trees and roses and had a two-story birdhouse that looked just like a dollhouse in front.

Meemie played the piano and sang, and Papa recited Shakespeare and spun fantastic tales about Ireland and the "little people." Tall,

Rose Cecil O'Neill Courtesy of Bonniebrook Historical Society

handsome, and a veteran of the Civil War, William O'Neill had a great love of books and was well-versed in the classics, art, and mythology. He was personable and outgoing, and it didn't seem to bother him that he was hopeless as a businessman. Rose's mother, nine years younger than her father, was both educated and talented.

When Rose was four, the O'Neills moved out of the quaint home William had built for Meemie. His bookstore and gallery had failed to make money, and the bill collectors were hounding him for payment. The Homestead Act, enacted by the US Congress in 1862, offered free land in the West to those who promised to stay on and improve the land for five years. Free land sounded like a good idea to a man who had little money. So the O'Neills loaded their books, furniture, and clothing into a covered wagon and traveled over a thousand miles to Nebraska.

The sod house where they would live must have been a big disappointment to William's gently bred wife. She had never needed to learn to cook or keep house, let alone farm. Now the family was on their own— away from servants and away from civilization.

William's ideas of living on the land seemed not to involve work. He would have preferred sitting in the shade reading poetry. But even a dreamer like William O'Neill had to come to grips with the price of groceries. His solution, he decided, would be to travel and sell great books to other homesteaders. Unfortunately, these hardy farmers who worked from sunrise to sundown saw little need for books, other than their Bibles. Meanwhile, Meemie spread her rugs over the bare dirt floor, learned how to milk a cow, and coped with floods and blizzards while William was gone.

By then, the family had grown to five; Meemie had given birth to Rose's sister Lee on the journey from Pennsylvania. It soon became obvious that other means of supporting the family would have to be found. Meemie got a job teaching at a school some distance away—far enough that she could come home only on weekends. So William became "Mr.

Mom," long before it was acceptable. He proved to be an entertaining babysitter, but Lee was unhealthy, and soon Meemie had to give up her job and come home.

In Rose's autobiography, she skips over these difficulties and does not explain how the family managed to live during the next few years. She wrote, "I (don't) remember how we came to decide we were not successes as agriculturists, but, it seemed, rather suddenly we abandoned the prairie and went to Omaha."

Rose was equally vague about her own formal education. Her father made sure the children were steeped in great literature and their houses were always full of books. Rose loved to draw. She entertained herself by drawing on any piece of paper she could find. William, who was years ahead of his time in discarding inflexible gender roles, fully expected his daughters to have careers and encouraged all their endeavors. Rose would later remember fondly how he meticulously whittled points on pencils so she would have good instruments for drawing and left stacks of paper in convenient places so she could draw whenever the mood struck.

Papa loomed large in the children's life; he was the life of their party. In contrast, Meemie seemed somewhat stodgy. She also seemed to take more control over the family's financial destiny during this period. Someone needed to do it—especially since there was now another O'Neill, Rose's brother Jamie.

Papa saw no reason for formal education for Rose. She was already far beyond her contemporaries in literature, art, music, and dramatic arts. Meemie argued that she still needed a conventional grounding in the more traditional subjects, like arithmetic. Meemie prevailed, and at age nine Rose was enrolled in a local Catholic school. Some of the other children made fun of her shabby clothes and elegant language. Rose was much more likely to spout a Shakespeare sonnet than the simple poems the other students memorized, and knowing *Ivanhoe* by heart certainly marked her as singular among her peers. Her life became easier when her classmates discovered she could draw, and they begged her to decorate their papers and schoolbooks with her illustrations of fat, funny frogs.

Although William still made occasional attempts to sell books and Meemie taught piano, the family, which with the birth of Rose's sister Callista now numbered seven, could never make ends meet. Consequently, the O'Neills had to move frequently, and Rose often had to leave school when the tuition came due.

Papa had decided Rose should become an actress, but she was much more interested in drawing. She pored over every art book in her father's extensive collection—not to copy the paintings and sculptures but to get ideas for different ways to draw the subjects. When she ran out of books at home, she checked out books from the library.

The *Omaha-Herald* contest marked a turning point in Rose's life. She'd worked hard on her entry, drawing a detailed study of a figure descending through rocky terrain. With its shading and shaping of hundreds of tiny pen strokes, her finished illustration was far and away the best piece of artwork the judges saw. Believing Rose must have copied the picture, they searched through art books looking for the source but couldn't find it. The judges then summoned Rose to the newspaper, where they tested her, making her draw while they watched. At last, convinced this little girl was indeed the artist, they presented her with a five-dollar gold coin. It was her first paid illustration and the beginning of her career.

About a year before the art contest, Meemie gave birth to Edward. He was a beautiful, happy baby, and his brothers and sisters doted on him—especially Rose. She cuddled and loved on him, carried him around, played with him, and drew pictures of him. The whole family was distraught when, at about two years of age, Edward got sick and suddenly died. The children planted violets all over his grave. Rose never forgot her darling baby brother, and a bit of Edward lived on later in her drawings of Kewpies.

Papa was still set on a stage career for his eldest daughter. Rose was fourteen, tall, and dressed in her mother's clothes when she auditioned for a comedy that was touring the Midwest in the summer of 1888 or '89 and was given a tiny part. The next year, she got a part with another touring company. In the meantime, her father had helped her land a couple of illustration jobs, and as she got busier with art, she abandoned the theater. During this period, the O'Neills added another member to the family—Clarence, known as Clink, the seventh and last of the O'Neill children.

By the time Rose was nineteen, she was busy drawing for editors in Omaha, Denver, and Chicago. It was time for the big city—New York. For a young woman to travel alone was uncommon then. Upon arriving in the city, however, Rose's reputation was well-protected because she lived in a convent run by French nuns. The sisters would accompany her as she made the rounds visiting editors and publishers and displaying her portfolio. The half-tone process, which made possible the printing of photographs in newspapers and magazines, was still in its infancy. Newspapers and magazines were illustrated with drawings, instead, and good illustrators were in demand. Rose was among the best and soon began selling her work regularly. She would never again live in Omaha.

Rose's family also moved again—this time to the Ozarks in southern Missouri. They were settled in two shabby cabins in the woods when Rose came home for the first time. It was a difficult trip. Springfield, the closest train station, was fifty miles away. Papa, Callista, and Lee came to meet her and helped her load her trunk and drawing materials onto a wagon driven by an old Ozarker. The ride to the O'Neill property was long, and the road got rougher and the countryside wilder. She was exhausted, and the very trees began to assume sinister shapes. Her wonder at the moonlit woods soon overcame her fear, though, and she imagined the tangled vines and trees to be peopled with fairies, elves, and all sorts of wondrous creatures.

After a night's sleep, Rose awoke to the wild beauty of the Ozarks. She wrote, "I called it the 'tangle' and my extravagant heart was tangled in it for good."

Although the cabins were rough, they were surrounded by roses and a little spring-fed stream that provided fresh water. One of the cabins served as the living area and bedrooms; the other was used for cooking and dining. Both buildings were filled with books, which were stacked everywhere. All of the O'Neills read voraciously. The family ignored the inconveniences and delighted in their woodland home, naming it Bonniebrook.

Rose continued to work while she stayed at Bonniebrook. A mailman on horseback came by twice a week, leaving mail in a sack hung on a tree at the mouth of the valley that led to Bonniebrook. Among the letters Rose found in the mail sack were those from a special friend, a young man she had met several years previously. Their courtship in New York had been carried out decorously under the watchful eyes of the nuns. Gray Latham came from a prominent Virginia family. His father was a pioneer in the motion picture industry, and Gray and his brother worked with him.

When Rose returned to New York from Bonniebrook, she brought with her many drawings she had done in Missouri. She sold almost all of them. She was working with increasingly more magazines, and in 1896, she became the first woman illustrator on the staff of *Puck,* a popular humor magazine. The magazine *Truth* published a cartoon strip she had drawn—the first published cartoon strip by a woman.

In the same year, at the age of twenty-two, Rose married Gray Latham. He was handsome and romantic and an entertaining companion. Unfortunately, he enjoyed his social life much more than working, and as the income from Rose's career increased, he seemed to make a career out of spending it.

Rose was supporting not only the two of them but also her family in the Ozarks. Always generous, she gave willingly, but Gray's attitude began to irk her. When she realized he was going to her editors and collecting her paycheck and spending it, she was disappointed and disgusted. After five years of marriage, she'd had enough, and upon returning to Bonniebrook, she and her father rode to the county seat in Forsyth, where Rose got a divorce.

While she was in Missouri, a series of anonymous letters arrived. They were filled with positive comments about her work—both her drawings and the stories she was writing. Rose was intrigued by the mysterious missives and surprised when, after a number of letters, her correspondent signed his name. The author was Harry Leon Wilson, her editor at *Puck*.

Harry was seven years older than Rose and frequently taciturn, whereas she was ebullient. The two shared ambitions to become novelists and, with that common goal, became engaged. They married in 1902.

Harry was a man of unpredictable moods—possibly suffering from what, today, might be diagnosed as bipolar disorder. One minute he could be charming and talkative, and the next, silent and cold. After a strange, three-month camping honeymoon in Colorado, the couple traveled to Bonniebrook.

Thanks to Rose's success, the house had undergone major changes, metamorphosing from caterpillar cabins to a fourteen-room mansion. The couple spent three winters there. Harry worked on his book, *The Spenders,* and Rose illustrated it. She also wrote and illustrated her own book, *The Loves of Edwy.* Both books were successful. The *New York Times* described Rose's book as "mystical and humorous."

In New York, Harry and Rose had many artistic and literary friends. Among the best were the novelist and playwright Booth Tarkington and his wife Laurel Louisa (who went by Louisa). Harry and Booth collaborated on several projects, and in 1905, Booth suggested that Harry and Rose accompany him and Louisa on a trip to Europe.

Again, their social circle included famous figures in contemporary cultural life. Their connections led to Rose being encouraged to send some of her drawings to the Beaux Arts Salon, a most prestigious annual exhibition in Paris. All of her works were purchased, and she was made an Associate of the Société des Beaux Arts, allowing her to exhibit in future salons without having to submit her work to the judges first.

Regardless of Rose's successes, when Harry and Booth were together, they belittled Rose and Louisa. The two women had their own defense: They invented "Wernicks." The name came from a furniture maker who had designed an expandable bookcase with pullout glass fronts to protect the contents. Louisa announced that "when our husbands attacked our characteristics we should have wings to unfold" to escape. The Wernicks had little skinny legs with rubber overshoes, gossamer wings, and a "hiney protector." Thus, when their husbands became too full of themselves and overbearing, the women called on their Wernicky senses of humor to deflect criticism.

Even with her Wernick defense, Wilson's black moods wore on Rose. After a while she realized, while on a visit to Bonniebrook, that she dreaded going back to New York City and Harry. "You don't have to go back," Meemie told her. So her five-year marriage to Harry ended.

Rose never married again. and she never had children. But she had babies—hundreds of naked little babies. Although she had occasionally decorated her illustrations with chubby cherubs, they didn't assume a unique personality until 1909. Rose invented the Kewpie—a little cupid, but spelled with a K "because it seemed funnier." She actually dreamed about the little creatures. "They were all doing acrobatic pranks on the coverlet of my bed."

The Kewpies, who were noted for doing good deeds in funny ways, first appeared in cartoons, but they became so wildly popular that manufacturers clamored for their endorsement. Kewpies sold everything from Jell-O to the Rock Island Railroad. Rose expanded their world, giving them their own village, Kewpieville. She added other characters, including Scootles, a baby tourist who frequently visited Kewpieville, and a pup called Kewpidoodle.

The popularity of the androgynous little elves with their tiny blue wings and wisps of blond hair on their mostly bald heads grew enormously. Children begged for Kewpie dolls to hold. So Rose became a doll merchant. Working with factories in Germany, she oversaw every step of the production process. Kewpies were produced in bisque china and ranged in size from tiny to tall. Rose won the hearts of factory workers when she complained that the smallest dolls didn't meet the standard of the larger models. "He ought to be the very best," she told them, "because he is for the poor children."

Rose had very specific ideas about society's rules and social conditions, and she used her illustrations as well as her Kewpies to make gentle points about justice and equality. Nowhere was this more obvious than in her passion for women's suffrage. While she made several public appearances, marched in suffrage parades, and even went to Washington, DC with a group of women from the New York State Woman Suffrage Party to meet with President Wilson, her greatest contributions to the movement came through her artwork. In addition to creating appealing drawings of Kewpies mimicking the famous painting, "The Spirit of '76," she drew more pointed works. Her drawing of "Sheepwoman" in the *New York Tribune* was accompanied by her opinion, "Man has made and ignorantly kept woman a slave. He has forced upon her certain virtues which have been convenient to him." She went on to say that women had a deeper understanding than men; "What she knows, man must figure laboriously through logic."

She also carried on her own quiet revolt against the strictures of fashion. "I was always rebellious against harness [corsets] and hairpins," she wrote in her autobiography, "and I cut my hair quite a while before the general cropping." She favored loosely flowing gowns and romantic fabrics.

The Kewpies made Rose a wealthy woman—freeing her to travel the world and to explore more "serious" forms of art. She was able to work more on drawings she called her "Sweet Monsters." Steeped in mythology and fascinated with the idea of the origin of man from animals, she created illustrations of robust, gargantuan creatures, which were well received in Paris. She may have been encouraged by the sculptor Auguste Rodin, and she later created several sculptures of her imaginative monsters.

By the early 1920s, Rose, while considering Bonniebrook her true home, owned several other properties. She kept an apartment in New York City, a country home in Connecticut, and a villa on the Isle of Capri. Always generous, she allowed her friends and many struggling artists to make her houses their homes—and some of them stayed for years. She helped finance her siblings' educations, and, of course, she supported her family at Bonniebrook. She also received many requests for help from strangers and often sent money.

Then the Great Depression hit, and people spent less money on magazines, books, and dolls. By the late 1930s, Rose realized she had spent almost all her money. After Meemie died, Rose sold her other homes and moved permanently to Bonniebrook. She began writing her autobiography, working on a new character, and planning a new doll. She wrote, "I don't know what came over me in these unmirthful times. But suddenly I had to make a laugh. I call him Ho-Ho." The new doll was a jolly Buddha-like figure. The timing couldn't have been worse. In December 1941, the Japanese had attacked Pearl Harbor, and no one wanted to produce a doll with Asian features.

Impoverished, Rose died on April 6, 1944. She was buried with simple ceremony at her beloved Bonniebrook. Callista, her sister and closest friend, sang. It was just as Rose had wanted when she told her sister, "I want my feet to face the creek because when it floods, it will wash my feet."

Rose Cecil O'Neill may be best remembered for her Kewpie, but her legacy is so much greater. She was an illustrator, painter, sculptor, poet, and author of short stories and a number of books for both adults and children. An advocate for justice and quality, she was also loved for her kindness and generosity. Fame and fortune didn't spoil her. Perhaps her finest tribute came from one of her Ozark neighbors: "I never seed nobody went so fur, and then looked back."

MARY ELIZABETH MAHNKEY

(1877–1948)

A VOICE FOR THE OZARKS AND
A HEART FOR THE HILLS

Mary Elizabeth Mahnkey lived in an isolated part of the country and saw beauty in the most ordinary circumstances. She wrote for love, not money, and left the world richer for it.

She came from a family of unsettled settlers. Her mother, Betsy, and father, Alonzo Prather, who was usually called Colonel, married in Indiana but moved to Arkansas, where the Colonel held several different government positions in several different towns. During that time he helped to establish the college that would later become the University of Arkansas.

The Colonel wanted land of his own, though, and so the family moved again—this time to Kansas. Although she was just a toddler, Mary Elizabeth remembered the trip. The covered wagon was packed full of furniture and trunks. Children Bob, Ben, Frank, Dick, Mary Elizabeth, and baby Joe now made up the family. The four older boys rode in the wagon bed with their little sister, while Betsy, holding her new baby, sat beside Alonzo on the wagon seat. "You children watch your little sister," Betsy told the older brothers.

The trip was long and tiresome. It began to rain. The creaking wagon wheels and the patter of raindrops on the roof played a lullaby. Soon the boys were asleep; Mary Elizabeth was not. Crawling to the side of the wagon where the cover was lifted for fresh air, she leaned out for a better look at the passing landscape. With a *crack,* the wagon jolted violently as it hit a bump in the road, tossing out Mary Elizabeth like a little

Mary Elizabeth Mahnkey These Were the Last: Townsend Godsey Foundation, all rights reserved

rag doll. When she fell, she hit her head and was knocked unconscious. Mercifully, the child was unaware as a back wheel of the wagon rolled over her hand.

The family traveled on. Eventually, Betsy noticed it was very quiet in the back of the wagon. Peeking in to check on the children, she discovered to her horror that her little girl was missing. The Colonel turned the team around, and the family retraced their route looking for Mary Elizabeth. About two miles back, they saw her tiny, still form lying in the muddy tracks. Picking her up carefully, they headed as fast as they could to a little town they had passed some miles back.

There, the doctor looked at the child's hand and shook his head. "I'm afraid we'll have to cut off these two fingers," he said. The child stirred and without opening her eyes, murmured, "Don't cut off Mamie's fingers." The doctor relented and bandaged them the best he could. The fingers eventually healed, although they were never as flexible as her other fingers and sometimes ached in cold or rainy weather.

That trip was the first of many for Mary Elizabeth—and she encountered many more bumps in the road along the way.

The family's stay in Kansas was short. Betsy hated the open prairie and the constant wind. The soil was not like rich Indiana dirt. Centuries of untilled prairie grasses had made a thick layer of roots and detritus that resisted the plow. Betsy was also afraid of the Indians, who sometimes wandered up to the homestead looking for food. So the family loaded up the wagon again and headed east for Missouri, settling in Taney County in the Ozarks.

Though most pioneering families in the Ozarks stayed put, the Colonel belonged to that strange breed of men who just can't seem to settle in one spot. The family moved frequently as the Colonel bought and then sold or traded their homes.

Betsy and Alonzo were well-educated, something they wanted for their children, but finding good schooling was difficult. In rural areas in those days, there were few standards for schools. Depending on the district, the school year could be as short as three months, and teachers were frequently only slightly more educated than their students. Consequently, a good portion of the Prather children's education took place in their own home.

Their parents placed a great deal of emphasis on reading. Mary Elizabeth learned to read before she went to school. She wrote later, "[B]ooks were scarce [in the area], but I grew up with the tattered remains of a grand old library that toured the Ozark hills with us." The family also always subscribed to the local papers, and they would gather around the fire on winter evenings as the Colonel or one of the older boys read the latest installment of a long story from the newspaper. Betsy journaled regularly; Alonzo sent local news to the county paper; and the children wrote stories and poems.

By the time she was ten, Mary Elizabeth had two little sisters, Adelia and Margaret, but her brother Joe, the closest in age to her, was her best friend and playmate. They created dolls out of corncobs, and fallen branches made great horses for galloping across the grass. Chicken feathers could be turned into writing pens, and they made ink by crushing the little round galls (growths) that appeared on oak sprouts.

The Ozarks were rugged and beautiful, but history had not been kind to the area. Before the Civil War, the hills had been havens for both anti- and pro-slavery factions. During the war, with many of the men away fighting, the women, children, and elderly were easy prey for lawbreakers. The lawlessness didn't stop when the war was over, and local authorities seemed helpless. Colonel Prather and several other respected men formed a citizens' committee to combat crime and to elect honest officials. The group, which became known as Bald

Knobbers, met atop the treeless hilltops (knobs), where they could see danger coming. Although the organization started out with good intentions, like many vigilante groups, it began to change, using fear and violence to gain its ends.

Colonel Prather left the group, which was officially disbanded in 1886, but some of the members continued to terrorize the area. Eventually, the violence subsided, but the children remembered the frightening night raids. The wild stories they told one another weren't about bogeymen; their monsters were Bald Knobbers.

By 1890, the Prathers were living on a farm beside the road that went from Springfield, Missouri, to Harrison, Arkansas. The children loved watching all the travelers that passed by. One day a family with several wagons and a herd of cattle and sheep approached, and the Colonel went out to the road to meet them. Originally from St. Louis, the Mahnkeys wanted to buy property in the area. Several children watched curiously from the wagon. Behind the wagon, several young boys prodded the animals to keep them moving. The tallest of these— blue-eyed, dark-haired Charles Preston (Pres) Mahnkey—smiled at thirteen-year-old Mary Elizabeth, who watched the procession from behind the fence. She didn't know it then, but she had just glimpsed her future.

Having been elected to the Missouri State Legislature in 1888, Colonel Prather was frequently required away from home. The Colonel had been a regular contributor of local news to the county newspaper, and now that he was traveling to Jefferson City frequently, the responsibility fell to fourteen-year-old Mary Elizabeth. She was also keeping her journal, where she wrote about friends, parties, and her desire to be a writer.

Mary Elizabeth had reached the point at which the teacher at the local school had nothing more to teach her. This was when the typical Ozark girl would get married and start having babies. Mary Elizabeth's father, recognizing her abilities, arranged for her to attend a March to June term at the Normal School (for teachers) in Bradleyville. The school was about ten miles away over the rugged Ozark hills—far enough that Mary Elizabeth had to board with a woman in the town. Being away from home gave her a new spirit of independence.

The experience helped prepare her for the challenges of her first teaching job. The school house was still under construction, and school supplies were nonexistent. In spite of this, she made it through the three-month term. Her students progressed well, and she won their hearts with her kindness and patience. Over the next few years, Mary Elizabeth taught at several other schools and added to her credentials by attending a month-long term at a teachers' institute.

While Mary Elizabeth was home one weekend, Adelia, one of her younger sisters, talked her into going to a dance at the Mahnkeys. The hard-working Mahnkeys didn't throw many parties, but when they did, they worked just as hard at making it a lot of fun. The boys were all good dancers and callers, and the girls looked forward to a great evening. Mary Elizabeth hadn't seen much of the Mahnkey family since she;d left for the teachers' school, and Pres had been away working, too. The last time they had seen one another, they were school friends. Now they were both grown up.

Soon after, the couple began courting. The Colonel frowned on the match; Pres had no money, no prospects, and little education. The young man had many good qualities, however, and Mary Elizabeth saw in him an honest, steady, hardworking man who would be a good husband and father.

Mary Elizabeth and Pres Mahnkey were married on January 18, 1899. They started married life on a rented farm near Kirbyville. The house was little more than a shed, but as she would always do,

Mary Elizabeth "made do" and made the place as attractive as possible. They had eggs, milk, meat, and a little money for staples, and the young bride couldn't wait until the ground was warm enough to plant flowers and a garden.

Mary Elizabeth was rarely able to plant roots, however. The young couple was fated to move often—six times in their first two-and-a-half years of marriage. There also were other adjustments. Mary Elizabeth had enjoyed her independence, but now her husband made most of the decisions, frequently without talking to her first. The couple eagerly anticipated the birth of their first baby, but she was born two months early and lived only nine days. The loss darkened Mary Elizabeth's life, and she suffered from depression, practically incapacitated with grief. Her sister scolded her, reminding her she still had a husband and could have more children.

After that, she put on a cheerful face, bottling up her sadness inside. But it was probably with a tinge of bitterness that she wrote:

I hunted a place where I could cry
Far removed from mortal eye
But Duty said, 'You must not weep
Go on back home, and dust and sweep. . . .

The next few years saw a succession of homes and farms. Some years went better than others. Their first son, Charles Douglas (Doug), was born in June of 1902. Pres was always trying to improve their circumstances—he bought and sold and swapped land and animals frequently. One of Mary Elizabeth's bitterest moments was when he came home with a new horse. He had traded the mare that had been hers since before her marriage—and hadn't even asked her. She wrote of her disappointment in her journal; she might be half of a couple but she was certainly not considered an equal partner. Anger did no good, and she accepted the situation as "the way things are." Another poem gives a glimpse of her feelings:

Contentment is a lovely flower
But it was hard to start—
It grows like resignation—
I can't tell them apart.

As busy as Mary Elizabeth was, she never skipped turning in a weekly news article for the county paper. People all over Taney County depended on the paper to keep up with one another, and Mary Elizabeth was one of many local correspondents. She wrote about local folks, neighborhood gatherings, and the changing of the seasons. She made people take notice of the little blessings of beauty all around them.

In 1905, a month after their daughter Roberta (Bertie) was born, Pres traded their farm for a store in Kirbyville, and the family relocated again. They lived in the back of the store. Pres' widowed mother lived on a two-hundred-acre farm just outside of town. Pres had owned the store only a few months when she decided to move out of state. Pres sold the store, and the Mahnkeys moved onto his mother's farm.

For five years the family stayed in one spot. Doug and Bertie started school, and in 1907, Reggie was born there. The Missouri State Traveling Library established a drop-off in Kirbyville, and Mary Elizabeth reveled in the supply of books. Perhaps they would have stayed on this farm indefinitely, but Mother Mahnkey still owned it and she decided to sell.

More moves followed. Pres bought and sold another store. Another baby, Bill, was born in 1912, while they lived on a little farm with a big lilac bush and tall poplar trees. Mary Elizabeth loved the place, but again, Pres became dissatisfied. She kept her complaints for her journal: "Pres is so blue it almost breaks my heart. I am discouraged with him. When he was in the store and making money he was so cross and so mean about everything I wanted done or any poor little thing I wanted to buy that life was so unpleasant. Guess he will always be that way." Pres, always so practical, failed to see much of what Mary Elizabeth treasured in life. She wrote later:

> *I have a dear, kind husband.*
> *He milks the cow, he hoes.*
> *But he does not see the butterfly*
> *A-swinging, or the rose.*

Over the next eight years, the family moved four more times—including a short stint in Washington state, where they hoped Pres and Doug would find good work in the shipyards. Tacoma had been a bustling place during the war years, but postwar production had slacked off and the Mahnkeys moved back to Missouri.

Melva, Missouri, was situated on the Missouri-Pacific Railroad line, and Douglas worked on the railroad. Pres had purchased another store, and the family settled in. Bertie helped in the business, and the younger boys were in school.

March 11, 1920, started out like any typical Missouri spring day—showery with intermittent heavier rains. When the boys got to school, they found it closed. The teacher had been unable to cross the rising creek, so Bill and Reggie had an unexpected holiday. Later, Pres sent them on an errand. While they were gone, the sky turned dark. Mary Elizabeth was fixing lunch; Pres looked out of the window at the clouds. He called to his wife to come see what looked like a waterspout coming toward them. "That's a cyclone!" Pres shouted. He and Mary Elizabeth ran outside, looking frantically for the boys as the winds grew stronger. They barely made it into the cellar, hoping against hope that Reggie and Bill had seen the storm and taken shelter.

The boys were down by the creek. They noise of the rushing water drowned out the sounds of the wind, and they didn't see the tornado until it was almost on them. They ran to a nearby house and got inside as the storm hit. The force of the tornado ripped the house off its foundation, throwing it into the swollen creek. Reggie was able to grab a willow branch and keep his head above water. He saw Bill being swept by and reached for him but couldn't catch his hand. He saw the fear in his brother's face as the water took him downstream and he disappeared.

As soon as the twister passed, Mary Elizabeth and Pres ran out to look for the boys. Melva was gone—the hotel, the store, their neighbor's houses. Their house, with the roof torn off, was the only one left standing. Neighbors who had escaped harm quickly began searching for those who were missing. Reggie was rescued. Bill's body was found late that afternoon.

The family was devastated. Bill's death left a hole in the family and a deep sadness in all their hearts. With their household possessions, their mule team, a cow, a horse, and about two hundred dollars, they left Melva, rented a place in Mincy, and started over. Mary Elizabeth abandoned her journal for the next eleven years.

By 1922, with Doug and Bertie both teaching and Pres farming, the Mahnkeys had recovered enough financially to buy a business comprised of a store, gristmill, blacksmith shop, cotton gin, and a farm with rich bottomland. Located in the community of Oasis on Long Creek, the site by a sparkling, clear stream with rising limestone bluffs on the other side was well-named. They lived in Oasis for fourteen years—the longest the family had ever spent in one place.

Mary Elizabeth had more time for her writing. In addition to her county column, she'd been asked to contribute a monthly column to the *Springfield News Leader*. She entered contests, wrote poetry, and occasionally submitted pieces to other publications. While Mary Elizabeth's columns often included stories about local people, many of her columns were more philosophical reflections, and she often included her poetry. Occasionally, she would get a small check; usually, she received nothing, causing her to comment, "They don't even pay for paper or stamps!"

Her reputation as a writer was spreading outside of the county. Folklorists like Vance Randolph and May Kennedy McCord came to see her, as did poet John Neihardt. She became acquainted with fellow Ozark notables like Rose Lane Wilder and her mother, Laura Ingalls Wilder, and artist Rose O'Neill. The artist Thomas Hart Benton came to call, as well, and while he was visiting he made a pen-and-wash drawing of a country fiddler, which he gave to her. A local women's group also published a book of her poems to raise money for a library.

Meanwhile, Mary Elizabeth and Pres had a decision to make. For years there had been talk about damming the White River, which would put Oasis under water. By 1935, the value of their land was dropping, and they felt they needed to sell while they still could get something out of it.

Earlier that year, the editor at the *Taney County Republican* had encouraged Mary Elizabeth to enter a contest sponsored by a major publishing company. The Crowell company published a number of well-known magazines, including *Colliers, Farm and Fireside, Woman's Home Companion,* and others. For their magazine *Country Home,* the Crowell editors were looking for the best rural correspondent in the United States and Canada. More than 1,500 writers from across the nation submitted entries. Mary Elizabeth Mahnkey of Oasis,

Missouri, population twenty-seven, a writer for the *Republican,* circulation 875, was the judges' first choice. The prize was fifty dollars and a trip to New York City and Washington, DC.

Mary Elizabeth met the mayor of New York City and Al Smith, a Democratic candidate for president, and she was interviewed on national radio. If the big city reporters who gathered around her had preconceived notions about this grandmotherly little lady from the backwoods of Missouri, they had to adjust their thinking. Her clothes may not have been modish, but intellectually, she was as up-to-date as any of her interviewers. She gained further respect from the journalists when she explained her philosophy: "To tell the truth kindly, to remember that mankind's chief interest is man, and to read over my copy and scratch out most of the adjectives."

She returned from her trip not to the Long Creek home in Oasis but to a small house east of Forsyth. She came home with a contract from *Country Home* for twelve columns for twenty-five dollars each.

During the next ten years, Mary Elizabeth moved three more times. She continued her writing for the county and city papers, and she enjoyed visits from her grandchildren. In 1943, she was named "Poet Laureate of the Ozarks" by a Springfield radio station.

Her arthritis was getting worse, and by early 1948, she was experiencing serious back aches. Diagnosed with cancer, she died on August 13—a Friday.

Mary Elizabeth Mahnkey had written for newspapers for fifty-seven years—publishing almost three thousand columns. Her hundreds of poems sang of everything from spring and butterflies to shame and grief. She raised and lost children and taught them to appreciate the tiniest things—"smart weed and beggar lice" and "a frost-bitten leaf." She loved and followed her husband through almost forty moves.

After her death, Doug's son Pat walked into his grandparents' bedroom to see his grandfather holding some of Mary Elizabeth's writing. With tears streaming down his face, Pres said, "I never knew she could do all this."

MARY TIERA FARROW

(1880–1971)
DEAN OF WOMEN LAWYERS

"What is this thing called love?" asked Tiera Farrow of a jury listening to her closing arguments in the biggest case of her career. Her client, Clara Schweiger, was accused of murdering her husband, Louis.

Did she do it? Without a doubt. Clara had been at the Jackson County courthouse in Kansas City arguing against her husband's petition for divorce, an action that not only had ended their marriage but had also deprived her of her son. The judge had just denied her request to set aside the divorce. Clara had encountered her now ex-husband and his attorney as she left the courtroom. Screaming at Louis Schweiger, she fired a number of shots at him.

Now, clutching at Tiera, she cried, "I loved him! My darling! My darling!"

The murder trial turned into a media sensation, with headlines playing up the unusual circumstance of a woman criminal and a woman lawyer. This was 1915, and the first time anything like this had ever occurred in the state of Missouri.

Mary Tiera Farrow (known as Tiera) defended her client's action as a result of temporary insanity. She began her summation with a catalog of famous love stories, claiming that throughout history, love had either ennobled or enslaved its subject. She told of Clara's tragic life and her delicate physical condition. She described the financial and emotional distress caused by the divorce:

> Gentlemen of the Jury [and it must be stated that women were
> not allowed to serve on juries in that day]," she pled, "stop and

Mary Tiera Farrow Courtesy of the Wyandotte County Historical Museum, Bonner Springs, KS

ask yourselves why this poor woman is here today. And you cannot fail to hear the answer—because she loved too dearly! She has fulfilled the law of womanhood just as God intended every woman should do, when she loves once and deeply.

She concluded, in a voice choked with emotion:

I am only a woman—first, last, and all the time—a woman just as Mrs. Schweiger is, and I am standing before you today pleading, pleading, pleading for the life and liberty of this poor woman....I trust that the same Great Hand that has guided me, will guide you twelve men, good and true—men who have seen life in all its phases, and that you will bring in a true and just verdict of not guilty.

Was Tiera successful? No and yes. The jury found Clara Schweiger guilty of second-degree murder. A finding of first-degree murder would have meant the death penalty or life imprisonment. Clara was sentenced to fifteen years in the state penitentiary. She served two years, and then was paroled because of ill health.

Tiera had begun her fascination with the law early in life. Born in Indiana, she had moved with her family to Kansas when she was five years old. There, her father ran a store and Tiera often helped out. She loved listening to the stories swapped by customers relaxing around the pot-bellied stove. One name came up frequently—Abraham Lincoln. A local banker was the son of Grace Bedell Billings, who, as a little girl in New York State, wrote to Abraham Lincoln, then a candidate for President, telling him he would look better if he let his whiskers grow. Lincoln wrote back and even visited with the eleven-year-old girl when his inaugural train passed through her town. It was a brush with fame that townsfolk never forgot.

The more Tiera learned about the late president, the more she admired and wished to emulate him. She later wrote in her autobiography, "His life had become an example and an incentive to me."

The third of ten children, Tiera was an enterprising lass from an early age. As a pre-teen, she set up an ice cream parlor in a small building next to her father's store. She got her first experience in labor relations, as she had to negotiate with her sisters, giving them a portion of the profits in return for their taking over her share of chores at home.

Upon graduation from high school, her childhood dream of becoming a lawyer like her hero, honest Abe, seemed as distant as ever. Instead, she moved from her small Kansas town to Kansas City and attended secretarial school, eventually obtaining a position in one of the large grain companies in the area.

If she'd ever had any illusions of equality, they were quickly quashed. She worked harder, was paid less, and had to dress in uncomfortable, confining clothes, while in the hot summers, her male co-workers removed their coats and rolled up their sleeves. Inevitably, she wished for a legal remedy to her situation and became more determined than ever to become a lawyer and an advocate for women.

That door was difficult to open. Law schools and colleges to which she sent inquiries replied that they did not admit women. Yet, Tiera knew that female lawyers existed. With pleasure, she discovered a new school, right in Kansas City, to which she had not yet applied.

The Kansas City School of Law, established in 1895, was unusual in that it targeted students who had neither time nor money to attend traditional schools. Classes were held in the evenings, making it possible to hold a job and still attend class. Tiera presented herself to the registrar and asked, hopefully, if they enrolled women students. Although he did not give her a definite answer, the registrar did admit she fulfilled the entrance requirement—a high school diploma. His first concern was that she, as a woman, would be traveling alone in the city at night—surely no "nice" girl would do that. His second concern was whether she could pay the enrollment fee. The answer to the second concern was an unequivocal "Yes!" To his first objection, she gave an evasive answer that could have implied a brother or father would escort her to class. These matters settled, Mr. Borland, the registrar and one of the school's founders, gave her a receipt for her fee, a brochure about the school, and the starting date for her class.

With some anxiety but a high heart on that first night of class in 1901, Tiera walked into a smoke-filled room and joined her classmates—all men—to begin her education in law. The men soon accepted her as one of the boys—almost. Her professors suggested she skip the criminal law sessions, as they might upset her delicate sensibilities. A classmate also occasionally reminded her, in jest, of the legal "rule of thumb," which stated that a wife could be beaten by her husband as long as the stick was no bigger in diameter than his thumb!

Tiera loved the study of law, even though its inequities frequently distressed her. She fumed at the idea that a married couple was considered one entity—with the man being the one. In one state, the law declared that a man could will his children to someone other than his wife. Her studies made her even more determined to use her knowledge to serve her sex.

Her two years of study had not been easy, as she worked at the grain company during the day and went to class and studied at night. Even the weather conspired against her. In the spring of 1903, rains caused the Kansas and Missouri Rivers to flood, washing out bridges between Tiera's Kansas City, Kansas, home and the school on the Missouri side. As the water began to subside, boats, manned by men who had to watch for floating debris, ferried determined people across the flood. Tiera was determined! On June 10, after a harrowing trip across the river, she received her first college degree—a bachelor's of law.

Alas, the legal world was not as thrilled. Her first legal job paid less money than she had earned at the grain company. Most of her work at

Dail and Carter was stenographic—typing up legal documents—but she occasionally accompanied one of the partners to court and was learning a great deal about the practice and procedures of the profession. She also was admitted to practice in federal and state supreme courts—although most of her appearances involved submitting paperwork or requesting a continuance for the partners.

When the partnership of Dail and Carter dissolved, Tiera stayed with Mr. Carter, continuing to serve as his stenographer as well as performing that service for another lawyer in the same building. She also answered questions from reporters looking for news. One of them, Tim Murphy of the *Kansas City Star,* suggested Tiera run for the office of Kansas City, Kansas, treasurer. Although women had not been granted the vote nationally, women in Kansas could vote in municipal and school board elections.

Tiera, who now had her own home on the Kansas side of the state line, certainly qualified. Murphy persisted, even talking her up to local Republican leaders. Pushed into running, Tiera entered the campaign with the intent to win. Her opponent, Miss Chadborn, made public appearances, where she sang to entertain her audience. Tiera made speeches about issues and her abilities.

The campaign was nothing like the mud-slinging contests that were common then. Tiera was quoted in the *Star* saying:

> *If I win, I want to win in a good clean fight. I think Miss Chadborn, my opponent, is a jolly good fellow and I wouldn't say anything about her for the world. But, I'll tell you something. I had to buy a brand new Easter-creation hat yesterday because she was dressing up so fine. I won't have it said that she can best me even in the art of dressing.*

Tiera combined her intelligence with a keen sense of humor, which often served her well in difficult circumstances. At one appearance, as she rose to step up to the speaker's podium, she tripped and fell flat. After the event chairman quickly helped her stand and recover, Tiera quipped to the audience, "That's how I'll come in—head first—on election day." Her quick wit eased the audience's embarrassment for her and won votes at the same time.

She served two terms as treasurer of the city of ninety thousand but declined a third term to fulfill another goal: Tiera longed to travel. She had been saving money for several years, planning carefully for an extended stay. In the spring of 1911, when her term expired, she was ready.

Even with a detailed itinerary, she found that circumstances altered her schedule. On the boat from New York to Naples, she made the acquaintance of a group of fellow travelers. One, embarking on a trip across North Africa, invited Tiera and several others to join him. Starting in Algeria, the group proceeded by train, then across part of the Sahara Desert by camel. Camping in the desert, wading in a small pool by the dunes, being chucked under the chin by an Arabian government guide who proclaimed her, "Very pretty, very nice," Tiera took her adventure in stride—quite a feat for a young woman in those days.

At last, she and a traveling companion returned to their more conventional itinerary. Tiera was enthralled with Italy—the colors of Naples, the art galleries in Florence, Rome's churches, the canals of Venice—but her trip had a serious purpose, too. She wanted to explore the status of women in all the countries she visited.

In Italy, women had no legal or economic equality, and lower-class women were little better off than slaves or beasts of burden. Women in Switzerland had better educational opportunities, but men controlled the property and children. Some German women worked as clerks or waitresses in the cities, but men ruled the home and their wives and children. In France, the situation was very similar. Holland, governed by a queen, seemed a bit fairer.

England's legal history fascinated Tiera. Little did she know, as she visited the historic Inns of Court, that one day the then-nonexistent University of Missouri at Kansas City's law school would adopt the Inns of Court concept (i.e., law students are divided into small groups with a faculty mentor) and one of the inns would be named for her!

Continuing her tour, Tiera visited Scotland, Ireland, Norway, Sweden, Finland, and Russia. She spent several months in Riga, then part of Russia and now the capital of Latvia, where she stayed with a cousin. While there, she studied German, attended a dancing class, and was wooed by a Russian noble. What adventures she had! But now it was time to return to Kansas City, and she was more determined than ever to help women achieve equality through the active practice of law.

Again, she found no interest in hiring a woman lawyer among the approximately eight hundred male lawyers then practicing law in Kansas City, Missouri. Her law school professors advised opening her own office and suggested another recent woman graduate as a possible partner. So it was that in 1912 the first firm of women lawyers in Kansas City was born. The shingle read DONAHUE & FARROW, ATTORNEYS-AT-LAW.

Tiera sold her Kansas home to help start the firm. The women soon discovered that clients were as difficult to come by as jobs. Not only were men prejudiced against them, women, too, doubted their competence. Most of their cases were small, and when they appeared in court, it was in smaller courts. To keep expenses down, they brought their lunches and prepared tea in the office.

The women did a good job of keeping up appearances, but the small fees they were earning were not meeting their expenses. Finally, a job as a county court reporter in Oklahoma became available, and the partners decided that one of them should take it while the other kept the office open. Tiera, having no family in Kansas City, decided to go, but both women agreed to keep the arrangement secret so no one would know they were hurting financially. When the Oklahoma court was in recess,

Tiera would hurry back to Kansas City, allegedly on out-of-town "law business," and when she returned to Oklahoma, no one was the wiser.

Finally, after almost two years of partnership, Anna Donahue called it quits and Tiera was on her own. Having put aside some money from her court reporter job, she was able to move to a smaller office. She struggled along, writing wills and taking whatever cases she could find. Then, in May 1915, a tall, thin, washed-out woman named Clara Schweiger came to her door.

She wept frequently as she told Tiera that her husband had obtained a divorce and taken custody of their adopted son. She talked of her nervous constitution and the "unfair and harsh" treatment she had received at her husband's hands. Yet, she declared, she loved him and wanted him—and their son—back. Tiera explained the appeal process and accepted Clara as a client. It was this case that brought Tiera Farrow to the general public's attention.

Following the sensational murder trial, Tiera was treated with more respect by the legal community, and she began to see more clients—particularly those seeking divorces. Divorce was becoming so common in Kansas City that the city was being referred to as the "Reno of the Middle West." This concerned both city leaders and the legal profession. Through the court system, proctors were appointed to study the problem and investigate divorce actions to determine the cause of the increase. Tiera Farrow was named one of the proctors.

She was now in demand as a speaker. As a proctor, she found that the stated causes of divorce were rarely the actual causes. Real causes included unrealistic expectations of marriage, money difficulties, and intimate details of the relationship that were embarrassing to discuss publicly. She related to audiences that husbands were rarely made responsible for supporting their wives and children, and little effort was made to reconcile feuding couples. She pointed out that over a quarter of all court actions were divorce cases and advocated for a Court of Domestic Relations.

She served several terms as a proctor, being appointed by two different presiding judges. The third judge was a bachelor who saw no need for the effort and discontinued the program. The number of divorce cases again began to rise.

Nineteen-seventeen was a momentous year for the nation and for the lady lawyer. The United States declared war on Germany, joining in the fighting that had been raging in Europe for several years. As her part in the war effort, Tiera joined with a group of young women to recruit young men for service. They would "raid" dance halls and clubs looking for likely candidates. The women were all young, attractive, and very successful in their quest. Tiera was given a special award for her service.

This was also the year that Tiera and some other female lawyers founded the Women's Bar Association of Kansas City. Barred from joining the men's professional group, they started their own. Tiera had also returned to Kansas City Law School for refresher classes.

That same year she met and married a handsome Latin American widower. The marriage was short-lived, ending in divorce. Though Tiera mentions the incident in her autobiography, she doesn't even give his name.

Following her successful efforts at recruiting for the military, Tiera decided to do more to aid her country and traveled to New York to look for other opportunities. She found a position as a stenographer in the US District Attorney's office. Some of the paperwork, especially dealing with spy cases, was interesting, but Tiera was looking for more action.

She quit that job and became an ambulance driver in the National League of Women's Service. Wearing a uniform, she undertook a number of tasks in the Motor Corps, including working with the Secret Service to deliver questionable diplomats and spies to the docks for deportation. She also met troop ships bring wounded servicemen home from the battlefront. She was preparing for overseas duty when the Armistice was declared.

With a settlement from her divorce and at loose ends, Tiera decided to go college to earn a degree in political science and sociology. She subsequently went on to Columbia University in New York, from which she received a master's degree in the same fields. Following graduation from Columbia, she took a short-term job with the American Institute of Criminal Law and Criminology taking surveys designed to be the basis of the modernization of the criminal justice system. A lifelong learner, she later added summer courses at the Sorbonne in Paris and at Oxford University in England.

Returning to Kansas City in 1925, Tiera began to reestablish her law practice. The Nineteenth Amendment, giving the vote to women, had passed in 1920. Tiera began speaking regularly to women's organizations about the law and the legal system. With lawyer Louise Byers, whom she had met when she returned to law school in 1917, she discussed the need for legal education for women—not to learn the practice of law but to learn of their legal rights. Both the granting of the vote and the experience women had gained during World War I opened new opportunities for women, and Tiera and Louise wanted to help them take full advantage of them.

In 1928, the Kansas City (Missouri) City Manager appointed Tiera a judge in the North Side Division of the Municipal Court—the first woman to serve in that position. She also returned to law school again—this time to earn her master's degree in law.

The world turned upside down in October 1929, with the collapse of the stock market and the beginning of the Great Depression. Students could no longer afford the women's law school, and Tiera was forced to close her practice for lack of clients.

With her background in sociology, she took a job first as a social worker with the Provident Association—a group affiliated with the Federal Emergency Relief Fund. With her legal training, she was soon promoted to legal case work. In 1943, she was appointed a legal aid counselor at the Legal Aid Office of the city welfare department.

After the attack on Pearl Harbor in 1941, the United States went back to war. Again, desiring to be useful, Tiera attempted to join the Women's Auxiliary Army Corps (WAACs) and the Women Accepted for Volunteer Emergency Services (WAVES), which was affiliated with the US Navy. Now in her sixties, Tiera was considered too old. She contented herself with making bandages with other Red Cross volunteers, but as the war went on, the government became aware of the increased needs for legal services for servicemen and their families. Tiera, working through the Legal Aid Office, was involved in providing that service.

Tiera continued to work for the welfare department until her retirement in 1957, and she also served several terms as Missouri Representative to the National Association of Women Lawyers. In 1950, she was admitted to practice in the US Supreme Court. In that same decade, she was first called the "Dean of Women Lawyers." Three years later, in 1953, her autobiography, *Lawyer in Petticoats,* was published. In concluding her book, she noted the changes she had seen in the legal profession, in the lives of women, and in the world—some of which she had helped cause herself. Through it all, Tiera had maintained her love of the law—even though it was a tough taskmaster and the financial rewards were small. The largest fee she ever collected was two hundred fifty dollars. In spite of that, Tiera looked at the accomplishments of the women who followed her and considered herself successful and her time well-spent.

Always modest, Tiera summed up her own achievements: "There never was a time, since I entered my profession, when anything topped the law as an object of my intense interest. Not for a moment have I ever considered myself a brilliant student; rather, I believe, I have been a consistent plugger. . . . My youthful dreams have served their purpose well. . . . What a wonderful day! What a wonderful world!"

Mary Tiera Farrow died at the age of ninety-one in a nursing home in Lenexa, Kansas. She is buried in Garnett, Kansas, with other members of her family.

From the time she enrolled in law school until she wrote her book, the ranks of women in law had grown from less than two hundred to over four thousand. By 1953, women were appearing in courtrooms as practicing attorneys and judges, and one woman sat on the US Circuit Court of Appeals. How thrilled Mary Tiera Farrow would be today to see women on the US Supreme Court.

NELL DONNELLY REED

(1889–1991)
READY-TO-WEAR REVOLUTIONARY

"**D**ear Paul, These men say they want $75,000. . . . if this is reported to the police you will not see me again." These words were written in a shaky hand by a frightened Nell Donnelly to her husband.

Mrs. Donnelly was one of the wealthiest businesswomen in Kansas City in 1931. Her chauffeur, George Blair, had just pulled the green Lincoln into the driveway of her home when it was blocked by another car. Several men surrounded the Lincoln, forcing George out of the driver's seat. The kidnappers drove George and Mrs. Donnelly into the country near Bonner Springs, Kansas, where she was forced to write the note to her husband.

When Nell failed to return home as expected, Paul, who was ill, had frantically called Nell's office and their acquaintances. He tried to reassure himself that she had simply been called away on business or had sent him a message that had gotten sidetracked.

The next morning he received a call from one of the company's lawyers; ransom notes had arrived there. The kidnappers had demanded seventy-five thousand dollars and threatened to blind Mrs. Donnelly and kill the chauffeur if demands were not met or authorities were notified.

The lawyer, James Taylor, called his law partner, former US Senator James A. Reed, who was not only one of the Donnellys' lawyers but also a friend and neighbor. Reed's abrupt departure mid-trial from a Jefferson City courtroom tipped reporters that something big was happening. Somehow, the word of the kidnapping got out, and reporters were on the phones to Kansas City editors before Reed could reach the city.

Nell Donnelly Reed Courtesy of Terence Michael O'Malley, www.nellydon.com

Upon learning that the story was already out, Reed issued a statement to the newspapers announcing that the ransom would be paid if Mrs. Donnelly was released unharmed. He added a threat, "If a hair on her head is harmed, I'll spend the rest of my life if necessary, seeing to it that the guilty ones are punished."

Kansas City in the 1920s and 1930s was a rough town with an unholy alliance between mob bosses and political figures. Stories differ as to whether it was Senator Reed or Chief of Police Lewis Siegfried who contacted Mafia leader Johnny Lazia. Whichever it was, the mob man was quick to deny any connection with the crime. One of Lazia's henchmen later reported that the police chief had threatened to shut down the city—booze, prostitution, gambling, everything—hitting the Mafia in the pocketbook if Mrs. Donnelly was not found.

Lazia marshaled his forces, sending scores of his men to comb the city for leads. After hours of fruitless searching, they finally came up with a clue—a restaurateur who had taken food to the hide-out. Several carloads of mob men descended on the remote farmhouse, brushing past the surprised kidnappers and grabbing Mrs. Donnelly and George. They drove the two shaken victims to a lighted spot in town and called Chief Siegfried, who immediately sent men to pick them up.

After police unraveled the story, three individuals were apprehended and sent to prison. Mrs. Donnelly went back to work at the company she'd founded—one that changed the way American women dressed.

Nell Donnelly, born Ellen Quinlan on March 6, 1889, was the twelfth of John and Catherine Quinlan's thirteen children. John was an immigrant from Ireland; Catherine, the daughter of Irish immigrants. Nell grew up in Parsons, Kansas, and upon graduating from high school, enrolled in the local business college. At sixteen, she moved to Kansas City to find a job, and in the process, she found Paul Donnelly, a twenty-three-year-old employee of Barton Shoe Company in St. Louis. The two were married the next year, 1906.

Sympathetic to Nell's desire for more education, Paul paid her tuition to Lindenwood College in nearby St. Charles. Following her college graduation, the couple moved to Kansas City and settled into the traditional pattern of the time—Paul went off to work and Nell became a stay-at-home housewife.

She had learned to sew as a child, and finding the garments worn at home by most women of the time to be drab, unattractive, and unflattering, she bought some pink-and-white-checked gingham and designed her own frilly, pinafore-style housedress. Neighbors and friends admired her work and begged her to make them copies of her colorful and comfortable dresses and aprons.

As more and more women called her for housedresses, Nell realized she had found a niche market. She was ready to expand. Packing up her courage along with samples of her work, she marched up to the marble and black-tiled building housing the George B. Peck Dry Goods Company in downtown Kansas City. The buyer was impressed and ordered eighteen dozen dresses to be delivered in two months.

Nell had to hire several women to meet the deadline. The dresses sold out immediately, and the store ordered more. Nell bought more fabric, hired more women, found a larger space to work, and within a few years, she had a debt-free, thriving business with eighteen employees and a quarter of a million dollars in sales.

In 1919, the business was incorporated as the Donnelly Garment Company. Paul was listed as president, Nell as the secretary/treasurer. Their titles didn't reflect reality. Paul handled the finances. Nell was the creator and innovator. Without Nell, there would have been no business.

Throughout the Roaring Twenties, the business roared, too. Demand for more styles and choices kept Nell busy with frequent trips to the fashion capitals of Europe to spot trends and to get ideas for new designs. But it was more than her ability to be on the cutting edge of fashion that made the company successful. She also incorporated production principles from other industries, like automobile and aviation, using assembly-line techniques perfected in large manufacturing plants.

While standardizing production techniques, she didn't subscribe to one-size-fits-all. She designed her dresses to fit a variety of sizes and shapes, and individual garments were constructed in such a way as to make simple alterations easy, with deep hems, adjustable waists and shoulder straps, and belts with sliding fasteners.

Her simple housedresses soon got dressed up and went to town. The line expanded from around-the-house styles to clothing for working women, as well as casual and sportswear for women. She didn't abandon the home front, though, and in 1925 she patented a clever apron—the Handy Dandy—which a worker could sew in one step.

Always looking for ways to produce clothing more efficiently without skimping on quality, she studied the textile industry. She worked directly with mills, eliminating middleman costs, and used cotton and rayon, sometimes known as "artificial silk," instead of pricier fabrics. Both she and her creations were now known as "Nelly Don," giving both persona and personality to the business.

Even the bursting financial bubble of 1929 didn't disrupt Nelly Don's success. It did, however, highlight Nell's concern for her employees. Since she'd started the business, her employees had been hired seasonally to put out the summer and winter lines. Knowing that many of her employees' husbands were out of work, she kept her factory running year round, concentrating on the Handy Dandy aprons during the off-seasons.

Although the business was successful, making the Donnellys millionaires, things were not going smoothly in the marriage. It would be easy to speculate that she not only designed the pants in the family, she also wore them. In addition, Paul's drinking was a problem, and he was a less-than-faithful husband.

The couple lived in a large, comfortable home next to James A. Reed and his wife, Lura. A former mayor of Kansas City and three-time US Senator, Reed had hoped to be the Democratic candidate for president in 1928. During his campaign for nomination, neighbor Nell Donnelly was one of his largest contributors. When Al Smith received the party's nod, Reed served the rest of his term as senator and retired from Congress, returning to Kansas City to resume his law practice with his partner, James Taylor. Among the firm's clients was the Donnelly Garment Company.

Nell came from a large Catholic family and had always wanted children. Paul was vehemently against it. In the summer of 1931, Nell and her niece Kate made a trip to Europe. Nell was going to adopt a child. She returned home with a baby boy whom she named David Quinlan Donnelly.

That was the story the world knew until 2006, when Kate's grandson, Terence Michael O'Malley, produced a film and book about his illustrious relative. In it, he revealed that the baby was actually Nell's, born at St. Luke's Hospital in Chicago—and David's father was James A. Reed. None of these facts were made public at the time. To the world, David was Paul's and Nell's adopted son.

David was just fourteen weeks old when his mother was kidnapped. This dramatic event was splashed over the newspapers and later stories appeared in popular crime magazines.

Less than a year later, Nell made headlines again, this time for filing for divorce. In her complaint, she stated that her husband had frequently been absent from their home and treated her with neglect. Paul did not contest the divorce. Nell bought Paul's interest in the Donnelly Garment Company, and the business was now truly hers alone.

Reed, whose wife had died a month before Nell's divorce, remained a close friend and neighbor. In December 1933, Nell invited a group of friends to her home for a holiday dinner. After the meal, she and Jim

Reed stood before another guest, a judge, and surprised almost everyone by taking their wedding vows. Nell's niece Kate was her maid of honor. The bride was forty-four; the groom, seventy-two. This was the beginning of a very happy period in Nell's life. She and Jim made a splendid couple, and Jim became a doting dad to David, whom he officially adopted. The business was thriving and so was Nell.

Jim enjoyed the outdoors—fishing and hunting—and the couple purchased a ranch in Michigan, where they could get away and enjoy the sports. Deer were plentiful on the nearly seven-thousand-acre property, and the family liked to fish in the lakes on the ranch. Not all of Nell's trips were strictly for relaxation. She sometimes brought employees with her, making it a working trip, but after work, she always took time for play.

Nell was recognized in the garment industry for her business acumen. Her insight didn't stop at financial matters; she was also concerned for the welfare of her workers and was ahead of her time in creating a employee-friendly workplace. Of course, in the beginning, her employees had been friends and neighbors. Her business was like a family, and it just kept getting bigger and bigger.

Nell wanted her employees to do their best, and she worked hard to find the things they did best. If someone was having difficulty in her position (most of the Donnelly employees were women), Nell would move her around until she found an area where she could be most successful. According to a family story, Nell fired only one worker and that was because the employee simply didn't want to work!

The list of accommodations Nell made for her employees was long. While working on concrete was standard in most factories, Nell's factory had hardwood floors. Coffee and doughnuts were available to workers as they arrived at their jobs, and in the afternoon, a lady came around with a cart with lemonade and snacks—the precursor of the coffee break. The company also had a cafeteria, and in 1937, when air conditioning became feasible, it was installed in the plant and offices. There was a dispensary with attending nurses and a doctor who visited once a week. The Donnelly Company was the first in Kansas City to provide hospitalization insurance and life insurance.

Nell paid tuition for any employee who wanted to take night classes, and she set up a scholarship fund for employees' children who wanted to attend local colleges. This was in addition to paying good wages. And she was assiduous about making sure employees were paid on time. One payday, which happened to be a bank holiday, James arranged for a local bank to open so that employees could cash their checks, giving them funds for the upcoming weekend.

Employees could buy remnants of fabrics at bargain-basement prices as well as "irregulars" or "seconds," garments with small flaws that made them unsuitable for retail sale. As if all these amenities weren't enough, Nell also purchased a farm where her workers could fish, hike, or picnic during their time off. Then, in 1937, she bought a three-story, stone home as an employee clubhouse. The house had a reading room, dance floor, and areas for other activities. She had several outdoor ovens built on the five-acre property. The clubhouse sat at the northwest corner of Swope Park, one of the country's largest municipal parks, giving groups access to even more space for activities.

Nell was into team-building activities before anyone knew of such a thing. Employees put on plays and participated in athletic activities. Every year, she held a giant Christmas party for workers and their children.

Meanwhile, Kansas City's garment industry was growing—in its heyday, becoming second only to New York City. It was never a capital of high fashion. Instead, local companies targeted middle America—the ready-to-wear crowd rather than the *haute couture* few.

In 1935, the state of the garment workplace was described as "the worst sweatshop market in the U.S." The International Ladies' Garment

Workers Union had been working to unionize the factories. Employees at companies that manufactured coats and suits were all union members by 1938. The dress manufacturers were the next target. The majority of workers at Donnelly weren't interested; they already had more benefits than the union could promise.

Union president David Dubinsky knew that he needed to break Donnelly, the largest company, in order to make sure the rest of the industry fell in line. Battle lines were drawn, and Nell and James prepared to take on the ILGWU. The union picketed the Donnelly Company. Nell's workers banded together and wrote their own oath of loyalty to her and the company. Of 1,300 employees, only six failed to sign the declaration. The workers voted to reject the union's attempts to represent them.

To Dubinski, the declaration of support was a declaration of war. He pledged one hundred thousand dollars to bring the company, the largest dress manufacturing business in the country, to heel. Among other tactics, he took out ads in major newspapers declaring that the employees were in violation of the National Labor Relations Act, giving the impression that Nell was resisting the union's standards for the workplace.

The workers took umbrage at Dubinski's accusations, with one commenting that it would take more than one hundred thousand dollars to make them yield. They also formed their own organization, which they called the Donnelly Garment Workers Union. The ILGWU upped the ante to two hundred fifty thousand dollars, and union officials contacted department stores that carried Nelly Don designs trying to persuade them to cancel orders.

In 1939, a federal judge ruled against the ILGWU and ordered that it must cease and desist in its efforts. That was just the beginning of an appeals and review process. The litigation that followed was complicated and involved several different parties, including the National Labor Relations Board. The legal battle ultimately wound up in the US Supreme Court. The company defeated the union efforts with a

Supreme Court decision in 1947. As long as Nell owned the company, its own employee organization was in charge.

The company's legal battle had lasted longer than another concurrent conflict—World War II. While the lawyers wrangled, Nell and her company worked harder than ever. Always the innovator, Nell looked at the needs of America's new work force—Rosie the Riveter and Mary the Manufacturer. All the quality she'd always put into her clothing was reflected in the work clothes she produced for women who found themselves filling jobs vacated by servicemen. This work was often physically demanding, even dirty. So she designed the dresses, skirts, blouses, slacks, and overalls for easy wear and care. Her efforts were recognized with two Army/Navy "E for Excellence" achievement awards.

In the midst of the busyness with the war effort, Nell suffered a great loss. Her beloved husband died at their Michigan ranch on September 8, 1944. Nell would describe the eleven years of their marriage as the happiest time of her life.

Nell, at fifty-five, was still in the prime of life. She continued to run her company, building it, by 1947, into the world's largest ladies' ready-to-wear manufacturer. Staying at the forefront of modernization, she began construction on a huge new building to accommodate the continually growing workforce. It incorporated the latest in heating, cooling, and lighting technology and covered two city blocks.

In 1956, after a half-century in the business, Nell sold her interest in Donnelly Garment Company. The company, which new owners renamed "Nelly Don," stayed in business until the 1970s, when the firm declared bankruptcy and ultimately closed.

Nell may have left the business world, but she was anything but retired from life. At sixty-seven, she still had lots of interests and energy. She enjoyed traveling and loved the ranch in Michigan, where she continued to fish and hunt. The interest she'd showed in improving the lives and working conditions of her employees now found broader outlets.

A strong supporter of her alma mater, Lindenwood, she established scholarships there, and on the local level, she served on the Kansas City school board. She sat on a number of boards of nonprofit, arts, and cultural organizations. She shared her love for the outdoors by donating over seven hundred acres of land to the Missouri Department of Conservation; the James A. Reed Wildlife Area was named in honor of the Reeds' contributions.

Her achievements were recognized with many awards. She received two honorary degrees: Doctor of Laws from Lindenwood College and Doctor of Humanities from Coe College. The National Federation of Republican Women named her Woman of the Year in 1977, and at the age of 101, she was given the Lifetime Career Achievement Award by the Career Club of Metropolitan Kansas City.

Nell Donnelly Reed died forty-seven years to the day after her husband, Jim. She was 102 years old. A woman of determination, energy, creativity, and intelligence, she shaped and led an industry. She worked hard and gave unselfishly. Her company may be gone and her fashions all but forgotten, but she left a legacy in the lives she touched and the land she loved.

JOSEPHINE BAKER

(1906–1975)

DISPLACED DIVA

One of the biggest stars in Europe, Josephine Baker arrived in New York City ready to take the city by storm. Women either admired her daring or shook their heads at her scandalous performances. Men threw flowers at her feet and gave her expensive jewels, furs, and even automobiles.

It was 1935, and Josephine had been away from the United States for ten years. An offer to appear in the Ziegfeld Follies on Broadway had brought her back. This tall, elegant black woman and her entourage swept into the St. Moritz, one of New York's finest hotels. Depending on the story, she was either flatly turned away or welcomed but asked to use the service entry. She later described the experience, saying, "America will not welcome home her own daughter."

"Depending on the story" is a key phrase in summing up Josephine Baker's life. Josephine herself told many different stories—some were false and she knew it; some were false but she'd told them so many times she believed them; and some were absolutely true.

It is true that she was born in St. Louis on June 3, 1906, to Carrie McDonald. It may be true that Eddie Carson, a drummer, was her father.

Josphine's childhood was full of unhappy memories—of scrounging for bruised fruit and vegetables behind the stalls at the Soulard market; of Carrie nailing flattened tin cans over holes in the floor to keep the rats out; of scrambling on top of coal cars to steal lumps of coal to sell for a penny apiece. Cold and hunger were constant companions. Josephine said later, "I started to dance to keep warm."

Josephine Baker Courtesy of the Missouri Historical Museum, St. Louis

But there were good times, too. St. Louis was a music mecca, and when Josephine could save a nickel, she would go to the local, black vaudeville house and imagine what it would be like to be on the stage dancing.

Her childhood ended at age eight, when her mother sent her to work for a white lady as a live-in maid. Josephine had loved the fairy tales her grandmother had told her, and now she was living one—Cinderella. Except she had no fairy godmother and no handsome prince. She slept in the basement with the dog. Her employer beat her frequently and once shoved her hands into boiling water.

By the time she was thirteen, Josephine was working as a waitress in a musicians' hangout called the Old Chauffeur's Club. She enjoyed clowning around with the musicians and occasionally sang and danced as they played. During this time she married for the first time, to Willie Wells. Even though Carrie signed her permission, the marriage probably wasn't legal. Josephine would develop a habit of being casual about the legalities of her marital state. The marriage didn't last long, and Willie Wells soon disappeared from her life.

While she was working at the Old Chauffeur's Club, she was spotted by a rag-tag trio known as the Jones Family Band. Worked into their act, she sang and did a little dance and learned to play the trombone. Her performances were completely spontaneous; not one dance was like the previous one. She played it for laughs, making faces and crossing her eyes. One night, an act that was scheduled to play at the local theater didn't show up. The manager called the Jones Family to fill in—and there was Josephine, living her childhood fantasy on the stage of the theater she had saved her pennies to sit in.

The entrepreneur who arranged the show found a place in his company for the skinny little girl with the googly eyes. It was her big chance and she took it, leaving St. Louis to tour with the show. In Philadelphia, Josephine met Billy Baker, a twenty-three-year-old Pullman porter who fell in love with her. Lying about her age and conveniently forgetting Willie Wells, Josephine married Billy.

Philadelphia was a great try-out town for Broadway productions, and Josephine tried to get an audition for *Shuffle Along*, a black musical that was being polished before its New York opening. Too young, the discouraged Josephine was turned away, but *Shuffle Along* was her new dream. She knew the show was perfect for her.

Leaving her husband and taking the train to New York, she again lied about her age and got a job as a dresser for the production. She learned all the routines, and just like in a movie, she stepped in when one of the show girls was sick. When she took the stage, she forgot all she'd learned, tripped over her own feet, and bumped into the other girls. She made it into a joke and people loved it. And Josephine Baker took a big step toward stardom.

Appearing in *Shuffle Along* led to other opportunities. Caroline Dudley, a wealthy black producer, was putting together a show to take to Paris and she wanted Josephine. Paris loved Josephine and she loved Paris. The stench of racism was prevalent in America, and France was like a breath of fresh air. Over the next few years, Josephine became the toast of Europe. She was dressed by the finest couturiers and strolled down the Champs-Elysées accompanied by a cheetah with a gold collar. French attitudes were much more relaxed than those in America, and Josephine, with her gorgeous body, often showed a great deal of it. One of the most famous images of Josephine shows her wearing only a tiny skirt made of bananas. Attitudes towards sex were also different, and Josephine had many lovers. Her comment was, "I'm not immoral, I'm only natural."

In 1926, she met "Pepito"—a Sicilian whose given name was Giuseppe Abatino. Although Josephine referred to him as a count, no evidence of royal lineage has ever been discovered. Pepito became Josephine's manager and lover. Eventually, she announced they were married—but that was as phony as his title.

With Pepito, Josephine left Paris on a tour of Europe that lasted almost two years. She captivated audiences all over Europe and in the largest cities in South America. By 1935, she was ready to return to America with a contract to appear in the Ziegfeld Follies.

Upon arriving, the blatant racism she encountered stunned her. Many whites thought she was "uppity;" many blacks thought she had forgotten her roots. Rehearsals for the Follies went badly; the show went worse. Reviewers panned her performances. Among the cruelest comments were those from the reviewer from *Time* magazine, "In sex appeal to jaded Europeans of the jazz-loving type, a Negro wench always has a head start, but to Manhattan theatergoers last week she was just a slightly buck-toothed young Negro woman whose figure might be matched in any nightclub show, whose dancing and singing could be topped practically anywhere outside France."

Many who saw her disagreed. Every night after the show, she appeared in the club she had opened, packing in fans who hung on every word she said and applauded wildly at each song she sang. She already had a contract as star of a new revue at the Folies-Bergère, and when the Follies run ended, she left New York.

Josephine, thrilled to be back in Paris, put all her energy into the new revue—driving the producer to distraction with her demands. The results were spectacular. In one scene, depicting a polar expedition, Josephine, wearing a ten-foot-long ermine cape, entered the stage on a sleigh pulled by a team of white huskies. She was glorious—at turns regal, seductive, funny, or poignant. She also had the ability to make each person in her audience believe she was singing just for him—or her.

She had a new hit—and a new love. In November, 1937, Josephine Baker married Jean Lion, a sugar magnate. With the marriage, Josephine became a French citizen—probably the best thing she got out of the marriage. She retired from the stage with the intention of being a wife and mother. That didn't last long. Jean filled her house with his relatives; she felt like a prisoner in her own home. So she committed to a fifteen-month tour of Europe and South America. While in Brazil, she filed for divorce.

By the time she returned to Paris, the continent was on the brink of World War II. In September 1939, France and Great Britain declared war on Germany, and Josephine was about to play a new role.

The French secret service needed informants—titled Honorable Correspondents—who could travel freely. Josephine's career made her a natural. Intelligence officer Jacques Abtey had his doubts, but upon meeting Josephine, he declared, "I found myself in front of a real patriot. 'France made me what I am,'" she said. "'The Parisians gave me their hearts, and I am ready to give them my life. . . .'"

In Paris, Josephine joined the Red Cross and worked tirelessly as refugees streamed into the city from countries already conquered by the Germans. But soon she had to leave Paris because the Germans had attacked France. She rented a chateau called Les Milandes in southern France, where she and Jacques carried on undercover missions.

Once, German soldiers came to the door, accusing her of hiding weapons. She invited them in with such charm and openness that they were disarmed and left without searching. She breathed a sigh of relief, as did the resistance officers she was hiding in the chateau.

She worked first with the French intelligence, but in June of 1940, France fell to the Nazis. A new government was put in place, and those fighting against the aggressors had to go underground. The leader of the resistance efforts was former Under Secretary of War Charles de Gaulle.

Josephine worked for the resistance in a number of ways. As a touring artist, she was able to travel to many countries. Sometimes she carried notes pinned in her underwear; other times, messages were written on her music with invisible ink. She also provided cover for individuals who needed to move from one area to another and facilitated contacts between the resistance and leaders in Britain and the United States.

When France became too dangerous, Josephine was sent to Morocco. While there, she became deathly ill and had to undergo a number of surgeries. She was incapacitated for over a year; rumors circulated that she was dying and even that she had died. At times Josephine herself thought she might die.

She was still very weak when she was asked to sing for African-American soldiers at the Red Cross-run Liberty Club in Casablanca, Morocco. The response was overwhelming and put Josephine on another path of service. She began entertaining regularly for American, British, and Free French troops, traveling thousands of miles, from Morocco to Egypt, camping beside the road, often sleeping on the ground, sometimes performing on a stage that was nothing but a few boards laid on the sand.

She raised the morale of the weary warriors and brought recognition to the Free French forces. For her efforts she was awarded the Croix de Guerre, the Medal of the Resistance with Rosette, and the Legion of Honor. She also had a new husband, Jo Bouillon, a bandleader who had also entertained the troops.

Following the World War, Josephine declared another war—on racism. When she was asked to appear at Copa City, Miami's largest supper club, she refused to sign the contract until the manager agreed that the audience would be integrated. The manager offered more money instead. Josephine was adamant—and she won. The show was a big hit. One of the observers was New York columnist and broadcaster Walter Winchell. The club was sold out every night, and as Winchell reported, "Josephine Baker's applause is the most deafening, prolonged, and sincere we ever heard in 40 years of showbiz."

Offers arrived from other cities, and as she wowed audiences with her art, Josphine campaigned for equality. In Las Vegas she not only got an agreement to integrate the venue but also secured hotel rooms in the resort where they were playing (formerly, black entertainers were housed across town and bussed in). She also called on Chambers of Commerce and leading businessmen, encouraging them to hire more blacks. In her honor, the New York City chapter of the National Association for the Advancement of Colored People (NAACP) declared May 20, 1951, "Josephine Baker Day."

Her efforts didn't always meet with success. The Stork Club in New York City was the place where "the elite meet to eat." The owner, Sherman Billingsley, ran the place like his own private fiefdom—which it was. Only the people he liked got in. He tolerated Jews but barred blacks. After one of her shows, Josephine met up with friends, and at the invitation of Roger Rico, who was starring in *South Pacific*, headed for the Stork Club.

Rico had been concerned about their reception but had been assured by several people that he could take Josephine Baker anywhere. The party was seated—and ignored. Drinks were served, but Josephine had ordered a meal that was inordinately slow in coming. When they finally got the attention of the waiter and asked about her steak, the waiter said, "There is no steak left." Roger Rico suggested crab cakes, only to be told, "There's no crab either." Before they could suggest something else, the waiter left. Josephine felt humiliated and left the table to call the head of the NAACP. By the time she got back to the table, a steak had arrived, but the disgusted party got up and left—and not quietly.

Sitting in the same room was Walter Winchell, the most influential—and feared—gossip columnist in the country. Winchell had been impressed with Josephine and had a reputation as a supporter of civil rights. Billingsley was a long-time acquaintance, though, and he provided Winchell with a ringside seat to the comings and goings of the city's most important celebrities. Winchell said nothing about the incident.

Josephine was furious at his lack of support and later publicly accused him of cowardice. That, in turn, made Winchell furious. In the meantime, the members of the NAACP and many from the theater community picketed the Stork Club. Winchell excoriated Josephine in his columns and on the air. He accused her of communist sympathies and even asked the FBI to investigate her. The feud damaged both Josephine and Walter Winchell. Concert contracts were cancelled, and the negative publicity made Josephine a liability, but the contretemps, along with the advent of television, helped to end Winchell's career.

Josephine again returned to France and threw herself into Les Milandes. She had grand and expensive plans for the property. It now featured a hotel with a swimming pool, an amusement park and theater, a wax museum of her life and sculptures of herself. By 1953, the place was doing well and providing jobs for local citizenry. She gave generously to the village, throwing an annual Christmas party during which all the children received toys and everyone got a present.

Never having been able to have children, Josephine turned to another dream—an interracial family. She began collecting orphans the way tourists collect souvenirs and between 1954 and 1957, brought twelve children into what she called her "Rainbow Tribe." She first adopted two boys, Akio, who was Korean, and Janot, who was Japanese. The boys were followed by two others, Jari from Finland and Luis from Colombia. Marianne was French from Algeria and Jean-Claude was from France. After Brahim, a Berber from Algeria, came Moïse, who was French with a Jewish background, followed by Koffi, from the Ivory Coast; Mara, from Venezuela, Noel, who was found in a garbage can on Christmas Eve in France; and Stellina, who was a French-born Moroccan.

The burgeoning family played havoc with her finances and her marriage. She had become very much the queen of her kingdom. She spent lavishly but would complain bitterly about bills and refuse to pay both her own staff and local merchants. She spent six months of the year on the road, leaving the children to be raised by her husband, governesses, and members of her family she had brought from St. Louis. When she was home, she issued orders to everyone. Jo, unable to corral Josephine's spending and treated like a lackey, finally left in disgust. The couple divorced in 1957.

In 1963, Josephine was excited about events in the United States, particularly the March on Washington, which she was determined to attend. Because of Winchell's accusations about her, it took President Kennedy and US Attorney General Robert Kennedy to clear her entry into the country. She marched with the crowd down the mall and was invited by Doctor Martin Luther King to come to the podium and speak—the only woman who spoke at the rally. Afterwards, she returned to France more determined than ever to make Les Milandes and her Rainbow Tribe a symbol of brotherhood.

Unfortunately, the cost of the expansions and the extensive staff needed to maintain Les Milandes were astronomical. Josephine's debts were too great, so the property was auctioned off and she was forced out of her home. Princess Grace of Monaco heard about her troubles and invited her to appear in the country's annual Red Cross Gala. Following that appearance, at the request of Princess Grace, Josephine was given twenty thousand dollars to make a down-payment on a small villa in Roquebrune, a few miles from Monte Carlo.

Josephine may have been down, but she wasn't out. She began touring again, including a triumphant appearance in Carnegie Hall. However, recurring health problems and the stress of losing Les Milandes took a toll. Over the next few years she suffered several heart attacks and a stroke. Each time, she bounced back—but each successive time, it took longer. Still, when she appeared on stage, energized by the adulation of the audience, she again became the star they'd come to see.

During this period, she visited a friend in Mexico, the American artist Robert Brady. Together they visited a church and exchanged vows with one another. It was an unconventional arrangement, a "spiritual" marriage rather than a legal one. The couple may have spent some time together but probably never lived as man and wife, and Josephine told few people about the union.

In 1974, she was again invited to star at the Monte Carlo Red Cross Gala. The revue featured scenes from Josephine's own life, among them a fantasized Louisiana childhood, her Paris debut, and her war service. The show was such a hit that she prepared to move it to Paris. It opened at the Bobino Theatre on April 8, 1975—fifty years after her first Paris performance. The theater was crowded with celebrities and well-wishers, many of whom stayed for an extravagant after-party.

The second night's performance went just as well. The after-party was a bit smaller but went on until three o'clock in the morning. Josephine was exhausted the next day and stayed in bed late—much later than usual. When one of her friends went in to wake her up, she was unresponsive. Josephine had suffered another stroke. She was taken to the hospital, where she died early on the morning of April 12 at age sixty-eight. As the crowds had gathered to see her when she was alive, they now gathered in silence to watch as the funeral procession passed the Bobino and drove on to the Eglise de la Madeleine.

Josephine Baker lived an amazing life, going from poverty and obscurity to wealth and fame. An entertainer extraordinaire, a war hero, and a champion of civil rights, she was alternately kind and rude, compassionate and demanding, generous and selfish—a complicated woman and a legend in her time.

BIBLIOGRAPHY

General References

Dains, Mary K., ed. *Show Me Missouri Women.* Kirksville, MO: Thomas Jefferson University Press, 1989.

Flynn, Jane Fifield. *Kansas City Women of Independent Minds.* Kansas City, MO: Fifield Publishing Company, 1992.

Phoebe Couzins

Morello, Karen Berger. *The Invisible Bar.* Boston, MA: Beacon Press, 1986.

Sanders, Matthew J. "An Introduction to Phoebe Wilson Couzins," Women's Legal History Biography Project, Stanford University, Palo Alto, CA, 2000.

Tokarz, Karen L. "Opening the Way," *Law School Magazine,* Winter 1990. Washington University, St. Louis, MO.

Waal, Carla and Barbara Oliver Korner, eds. *Hardship and Hope: Missouri Women Writing about Their Lives, 1820–1920.* Columbia, MO: University of Missouri Press, 1997.

Susan Elizabeth Blow

Harrison, Elizabeth. *Sketches along Life's Road.* Boston: Stratford Company, 1930.

Menius, Joseph M. *Susan Blow.* St. Clair, MO: Page One Publishing, 1993.

Primm, James Neal. *Lion of the Valley: St. Louis, Missouri, 1764–1980.* St. Louis: Missouri Historical Society Press, 1998.

Rogers, Dorothy G. "Before Pragmatism: The Practical Idealism of Susan E. Blow," *Transactions of the Charles S. Peirce Society*, Fall 2000. Indianapolis: Indiana University Press.

Ross, Elizabeth Dale. *The Kindergarten Crusade.* Athens, OH: Ohio University Press, 1976.

Cathy Williams

Hart, Herbert M. *Old Forts of the Southwest: 1850–1890.* New York: Bonanza Books, 1964

Myers, Lee. "Mutiny at Fort Cummings," *New Mexico Historical Review,* October 1971, pp. 337–350.

St. Louis Daily Times. "She Fought Nobly," January 2, 1876.

Tucker, Phillip Thomas. *Cathy Williams: From Slave to Female Buffalo Soldier.* Mechanicsburg, PA: Stackpole Books, 2002.

Virginia Alice Cottey Stockard

Campbell, Elizabeth McClure. *The Cottey Sisters of Missouri*. Arkansas City, KS:
    Gilliland Printing Company, 1970.
"Cottey College: A Century of Commitment to Women," commemorative booklet.
    Cottey College, 1984.
"Cottey: One Vision 125 Years," commemorative booklet. Cottey College, 2009.
Troesch, Helen DeRusha. *The Life of Virginia Alice Cottey Stockard*. PEO Sisterhood,
    1995.

Kate Chopin

Aubuchon, Bob. "Remembering the Gasconade Disaster," Central Pacific Railroad
    Photographic History Museum, http://cprr.org
"Kate Chopin," Kate Chopin International Society, http://katechopin.org
Toth, Emily. *Kate Chopin*. New York: William Morrow and Company, 1990.
———. *Unveiling Kate Chopin*. Jackson, MS: University Press of Mississippi, 1999.

Alice Berry Graham and Katharine Berry Richardson

Johns, Beatrice. *Women of Vision*. Wentzville, MO: ImagineInk Publishing Company,
    2004.
Kansas City Star Magazine. "She Spells Success the Old-Fashioned Way," August 3,
    1924.
Wenner, Herbert A. and Sydney F. Pakula. The History of the Children's Mercy
    Hospital in Kansas City, Missouri. Unpublished manuscript, 1984.
"Women in Health Sciences: Biographies: Alice Berry Graham (1850–1913) and
    Katherine Berry Richardson (1858–1933)." http://beckerexhibits.wustl.edu/
    mowihsp/bios/GrahamRichardson.htm

Laura Ingalls Wilder

Berne, Emma Carlson. *Laura Ingalls Wilder*. Edina, MN: ABDO Publishing Company,
    2008.
Hines, Stephen, ed. *Laura Ingalls Wilder Little House in the Ozarks: The Rediscovered
    Writings*. Nashville: Thomas Nelson, Inc., 1991.
Miller, John E. *Becoming Laura Ingalls Wilder: The Woman behind the Legend*.
    Columbia, MO: University of Missouri Press, 1998.
Wilder, Laura Ingalls. *By the Shores of Silver Lake*. New York: HarperCollins, 1939.
———. *The First Four Years*. New York: HarperCollins, 1971.
———. *Little House in the Big Woods*. New York: HarperCollins, 1932.
———. "Notes from the Real Little House on the Prairie," *Saturday Evening Post*,
    September 1978, pp. 56–57, 104–105.
———. *These Happy Golden Years*. New York: HarperCollins, 1943.

Zochert, Donald. *Laura: The Life of Laura Ingalls Wilder*. Chicago: Henry Regnery Company, 1976.

Rose Cecil O'Neill

Brewster, Linda. *Rose O'Neill: The Girl Who Loved to Draw*. Princeton: Boxing Day Books, 2009.

Formanek-Brunell, Miriam, ed. *The Story of Rose O'Neill: An Autobiography*. Columbia, MO: University of Missouri Press, 1997.

Scott, Susan K. "America's First Female Cartoonist Fought for Women's Suffrage," *The Ozark Mountaineer*, March/April 2010, pp. 5–10.

The Story of Rose O'Neill (DVD). Branson, MO: Bear Creek Productions, 2004.

Mary Elizabeth Mahnkey

Cummings, Dorothy, "Melva," White River Valley Historical Quarterly, Fall 1963.

Mahnkey, Douglas. "The Mahnkey and Prather Families," *White River Valley Historical Quarterly,* Winter 1970–1971.

Mahnkey, Mary Elizabeth. *Marigold Gold.* Lebanon, MO: Bittersweet, Inc., 1999.

Massey, Ellen Gray. *A Candle Within Her Soul: Mary Elizabeth Mahnkey and Her Ozarks.* Lebanon, MO: Bittersweet, Inc., 1996

Mary Tiera Farrow

Berry, Dawn Bradley. *The Fifty Most Influential Women in American Law.* Los Angeles: Lowell House, 1996.

Farrow, Tiera. *Lawyer in Petticoats.* New York: Vantage Press, 1953.

Flynn, Jane Fifield. *Kansas City Women of Independent Minds.* Kansas City, MO: Fifield Publishing Company, 1992.

Morello, Karen Berger. *The Invisible Bar.* Boston: Beacon Press, 1986.

Thirsk, Alyssa Eve. "Unearthing a Gem: The Story of Tiera Farrow, A Kansas City Lawyer," Women's Legal History Biography Project, Stanford University, Palo Alto, CA, 2000.

Nell Donnelly Reed

Ancel, Judy. "The Garment Workers," Talk for Kansas City Labor History Tour, October 17, 24, 1992. http://kclabor.org/garment_workers.htm.

McMillen, Margot Ford, and Heather Roberson. *Called to Courage: Four Women in Missouri History.* Columbia, MO: University of Missouri Press, 2002.

O'Dwyer, Tom. "Hot Cargo," *True Detective*, August 1943.

O'Malley, Terence Michael. *Nelly Don: A Stitch in Time.* Kansas City, MO: The Covington Group, 2006.

Snider, Amy, "Nell Donnelly Reed is dead at age 102," *Kansas City Star,* September 9, 1991, A1:3, A1:9.

Josephine Baker

Baker, Jean-Claude and Chris Chase. *Josephine: The Hungry Heart.* New York: Random House, 1993.

Haney, Lynn. *Naked at the Feast.* New York: Dodd, Mead & Company, 1981.

Lahs-Gonzales, Olivia, ed. *Josephine Baker: Image & Icon.* St. Louis: Reedy Press, 2006.

Rose, Phyllis. *Jazz Cleopatra.* New York: Doubleday, 1989.

Schroeder, Alan. *Josephine Baker.* New York: Chelsea House, 2006.

Wood, Ean. *The Josephine Baker Story.* London: Sanctuary Publishing Limited, 2000.

INDEX

National Woman Suffrage
Association (NWSA),
5, 6
Native American conflicts,
26–29
Nelly Don fashions. *See*
Donnelly Garment
Company
Nelson, William Rockhill,
60–61
Nightingale, Florence, 62
Nineteenth Amendment,
5, 110
nursing, 61–62
NWSA (National Woman
Suffrage Association),
5, 6

O

O'Flaherty, Thomas, 41,
43–44, 46
O'Neill, Alice Aseneth Cecilia
Smith "Meemie," 75,
77–79
O'Neill, Clarence, 80
O'Neill, Edward, 79–80
O'Neill, Lee, 77
O'Neill, Rose Cecil
acquaintances, 97
death and legacy, 85–86
early years, 75, 76–80

illustration career, 75, 79,
80–85
marriages, 81–83
portrait, *76*
O'Neill, William Patrick, 75,
77–79
*On the Banks of Plum
Creek* (Laura Ingalls
Wilder), 73

P

Philanthropic Educational
Organization (PEO), 40
pioneers, 64–74, *65,*
87–99, *88*
poets, 87–99
politicians, 105–6, 111
pregnancy, 47
Price, Sterling, 23–24
Provident Association, 110
Puck (magazine), 81

R

racism, 127, 130–31, 132
Rainbow Tribe, 132
ready-to-wear fashion,
116–23
Reed, James A., 113, 115,
118–19, 120, 121, 122
Reed, Nell Donnelly
awards, 123

ABOUT THE AUTHOR

Though born in Kansas and a longtime resident of Oklahoma, Elaine Warner has roots deep in the Missouri soil. Her early childhood was spent on both sides of the Kansas/Missouri state line, and her maternal grand- and great-grandparents were from Greene and Taney Counties in the southwestern corner of the state.

She concentrates primarily on travel writing, having been published in a number of newspapers and magazines. Her book, *Insiders' Guide®
to Tulsa,* was published by Globe Pequot Press and released in 2010.

A member of the Society of American Travel Writers, she blogs about her adventures at www.okietravel.blogspot.com. Her traveling companion, a teddy bear who is part of the organization's geography education program, blogs for children at www.teddietravel.blogspot.com.